A Guide to Bliss
Transforming Your Life through Mind Expansion

Shai Tubali

For more information, contact:

MSI Press
1760-F Airline Hwy, #203
Hollister, CA 95023
orders@msipress.com
info@msipress.com
tel. /fax: 831-886-2486

Library of Congress Control Number 2014948865

ISBN 9781933455945

Cover design by CDL Services.

Typesetting by Keshav Sharma

What People Are Saying about *A Guide to Bliss*

"For most people, true feelings of happiness are forever fleeting and tied to certain expectations. In that way, happiness becomes an experience that is dependent on other people and external circumstances. It's difficult to free oneself from these constraints since they stem from mental and emotional patterns that already started forming in our childhood. With the White Light, Shai Tubali has developed a method that we can use in order to expand into wider layers of consciousness. The book presents easy-to-apply techniques that connect us to our enlightened potential and integrates them with growing ease into daily life." — *Bewusstsein Magazine*, Austria

"This book makes you really want to try and work with the suggested techniques!" — *Spuren Magazine*, Switzerland

"Whoever touches the field of consciousness of the White Light, which gave the method its name, understands that the doors that lead back to our divine essence are wide open." — *Sein Magazine*, Germany

"I have tried the 'expansion process' which appears at the beginning of the book. Words cannot describe the joy that flooded me and the showers of insights. The process itself imbues [one] with a tremendous positive energy. Whoever manages to expand once will wish to return again and again to that experience. Highly recommended." — *Different Life Magazine*, Israel

"As a psychologist, I was surprised that I could find profound positive changes after just one session." — Anja Grossmann, psychologist, Austria

"I use the expansion of the White Light to help people transcend and touch higher levels of their being. One White Light process can equal ten other kinds of therapies. I especially love the White Light for negative memories which has a deep healing dimension to it in cases of loss and deep sadness." — Ilana Goldstein, psychotherapist, Israel

"These techniques are very good for many of my clients, for addiction, relationship issues, depression, issues of self-worth and anxieties." — Inke Jochims, psychotherapist, Germany

"The method presented in this book adds, in my mind, a significant layer to the growing synthesis between meditation and psychology as well as to the universal effort to understand and free the complex human mind. This method brings the harmony and benediction of ancient meditation to the doorstep of the Western practitioner, and turns the traditional practice into incredibly accessible and easy-to-use modern techniques." — Nir Brosh, Medical Doctor and Homeopath

Table of Contents

Preface

Fourteen years ago, when I was twenty-three years old, I underwent an intense, world-shattering expansion of consciousness for a few long months. It took place in the midst of a fervent spiritual search. Until then, my three years of seeking had granted me only brief glimpses into broader states of consciousness. Those glimpses far from quenched my ever-increasing thirst. This time, something else erupted within me, or so it seemed. This expansion, which permeated my entire being, did not dissipate, but rather grew day after day without any substantial effort on my part. It seemed like the only thing I was expected to do from then onward was observe the happening and not interfere.

Back then I lived at my parents' house. For a whole year, I remained enclosed in my small room, only leaving the house from time to time to wander about for hours and curiously examine my new relationship with the world. Of course, at that time I did not define what I was going through as an "expansion of consciousness," a term whose depth and significance will be clearly presented to anyone who reads this book, as I did not possess the proper terminology. In fact, words were too narrow and frail to contain the immensity of the experience for me, and my familiar structures of thought crumbled and collapsed under the heavy load of this new state. One thing was certain: the way I perceived myself and the essence of my being, my thoughts and emotions, my relationships and aspirations, was irre-

versibly transformed. In the vastness of these planes of consciousness, there was absolutely no meaning to whatever I recognized as
"myself" and "my personal life." There was only that boundless, infinite presence, all-embracing love, and fragrance of eternity which
accompanied me at all times and in all places.

At the end of that year, when I was twenty-four years old, spiritual seekers from here and there initiated communication with me
in the hope of being inspired by my new state. Slowly but surely, I
became fully absorbed in a new life of teaching and writing in the
field of spiritual development. Ever since that year, the central question that has kept me overwhelmingly busy has been: What makes a
person transform to the core of his being? What are the ideal conditions for laying the groundwork for complete transformation in a
human being?

One certain fact was gleaming before my mind's eye throughout
this journey: as if of their own accord, many mental and emotional
patterns that used to mold and condition my personality were disintegrating through the process of the expansion of consciousness day
after day. A state of joy and bliss, independent from circumstances
or any "other," was overflowing within my heart, and a new level of
fearless and wakeful listening was flooding my brain. This made it
obvious that a tight connection existed between one's stabilization
in vast states of consciousness and one's liberation from confining
psychological structures. However since I did not have the slightest
idea what exactly had brought about this process within my own self,
I did not know how to properly awaken it in others to the degree that
it would take root in them as an irreversible state, as a new stage of
consciousness.

Thus, through all of my years of teaching and writing, I sensed
that something fundamental was lacking in my communication with
those who sought a genuine change in their lives. A bridge was missing, something that would mediate between the "unreachable" state
of expanded consciousness and the ordinary state of consciousness, which is overwhelmed with suffering, conflict, and confusion.
The classical meditation techniques, as well as the mind techniques

which I attempted to use, did not bring about the much-sought-after results, and I myself was unable to discover an original solution.

Only five years ago, it became clear that this was a highly positive and necessary kind of frustration since this frustration drove me to develop the White Light Expansion method. As soon as I began trying out this method with those around me, I realized that the bridge had finally been created: whenever a person underwent the process of expansion, which is the heart of this method, we could meet in the subtle planes of consciousness and truly understand each other, owing to the common direct revelation. No one needed me as the mediator of these states anymore since a fully independent way to profoundly and continuously get in touch with them had been revealed. Much more than that: the method provided those around me with the capacity to go through a process similar to my own and to successfully shed stubborn patterns and psychological structures; we all tapped into the ability to apply the effect of the expansion of consciousness to many dimensions of life which are not purely spiritual—therapeutic or creative dimensions, for instance. Spiritual enlightenment had become useful for our everyday lives.

I did not mean to create a method. The White Light Expansion was conceived unintentionally experimenting with the fragments and principles of methods, meditation techniques, and mind techniques that I had come to appreciate throughout the years. While experimenting with these ideas, I sought new elements and principles that could enhance and deepen their potential for transformation. Techniques, such as, the *Zero Point Process* of Dr. Gabriel Cousens, Brandon Bays' *The Journey*, *The Work* of Byron Katie, the *Past Life Regression* of the Dutch school of holographic therapy and more were spread out before my mind's eye. On the other side, forever inspiring me, were the teachings of spiritual masters, such as philosopher Jiddu Krishnamurti's transmutation of the brain and the esoteric knowledge of the ancient Yogic tradition. Inspiration for the process of expansion, as it is presented in this book, was particularly drawn from the *Zero Point Process* of Dr. Gabriel Cousens, which is based on defining a structure and expanding it in order to clear away patterns, and from *The Journey* of Brandon Bays, which aims at discovering, within the depths of negative emotions, the bliss of consciousness.

This method, the White Light Expansion, quite rapidly began to develop and take on a life of its own, launching itself into unique skies full of possibilities. Its philosophical foundations became far more solid, and a few dozen techniques based upon the same principles were formed. Each one held within itself a transformative potential for a particular dimension of life. Thus, in a totally unplanned manner, I started realizing that the process of expansion is applicable to a multitude of life's dimensions. Accordingly, from one technique aimed at the transmutation of negative emotions, there eventually sprouted more than fifty other techniques. Among them were one (highly effective!) process for dream interpretation, another for the complete experience of the enlightened state, and a variety for creative decision-making in everyday life.

Nowadays, the White Light is a world unto itself, an invitation to an infinite journey within the expanses of consciousness, and undoubtedly, it has not said its last word. In my eyes, its greatest gift, before anything else, lies in its ability to inform us, by means of direct experience, that the potential of our consciousness is, indeed, inconceivable and infinite, and that, in actuality, we fulfill but a minuscule percentage of it. There exists within our consciousness an amazing scope of possible directions and actions—after all, being a human means, first and foremost, owning a consciousness—and through the expansion process, we are finally capable of realizing significant portions of it.

The book you are holding in your hands aims at enabling you to develop and cultivate the skill of the expansion process, which lies at the core of the White Light method. Further, it guides you to apply this process on your own to the various dimensions of life: from the therapeutic and psychological plane to decision-making and to spiritual and meditative elevation. In a sense, the very structure of this book is, in itself, a wholesome course of expansion; it goes from providing us with skills for coping with the mental and emotional world within us to giving us knowledge of healthy and constructive interactions with the world around us and then to giving us the ability to get in touch with the universe and the infinity that encompasses us wherever we go.

In order to learn the method and put it into action by yourself, it is important to obtain a profound and comprehensive understanding of the nature of the expansion process. For this reason, you will find a great deal of theoretical knowledge in this book. At the same time, you will find seven techniques specifically adjusted for self-work, from which you can pick to your heart's content, on your own free time and according to the present inclination of your heart.

You may perform the techniques in three ways:

1. With the help of a friend or a partner who will meditatively read the form aloud, thus creating for you a relaxed and easy-going space for the inner process. This is by far the simplest and most efficient way.

2. By recording yourself reading the form aloud, and then listening to the recording and following the instructions, either by heart or with pen and paper. You can respond vocally to the instructions, but if this is too odd for you, you can do it silently in your mind. This is an excellent method for self-work.

3. By directly working with the form: reading it, closing your eyes, and then putting the instructions into action. In this way, we also respond to the instructions, either by heart or in writing, vocally or silently. This option is recommended for the advanced, who have already undergone successful and swift experiences in the expansion process.

The purpose of this book is primarily to encourage you to fall in love with this process, which has already changed the lives of many for the better, and consequently, to urge you to practice expansion on a daily basis for the sake of ongoing contact with an inner state of limitlessness, bliss, lightheartedness, creativity, and radical freedom from suffering and conditioning. Each technique in this book is a world unto itself in which one can travel more and more. Yet, at the same time, it is perfectly fine to switch direction every day or to experiment from time to time as you see fit.

Should you find the White Light Expansion a potent method for profound healing and fundamental life-changes, it is likely that you will eventually seek an authorized White Light instructor, with whom you can be responsibly guided into a more meticulous and complex process. The techniques in this book are specifically adjusted for self-work, and for this reason, they are far shorter and simpler than those which the instructors have at their disposal. More than that, we often need someone who can observe us from the outside in order to attain a more objective perception. However, the seven carefully selected techniques in this book are, transformationally speaking, highly potent and hold within themselves opportunities for extensive journeys into the mysteries of the consciousness and its manifold possibilities.

Finally, I would like to convey my gratitude, from the bottom of my heart and consciousness, to Eilon Lester, the White Light Expansion founder, whose love of the method and complete faith in its significance drive him day and night to disseminate it in every way possible. I would also like to thank Eilon Lester's passionate supporter, Noga Sinai, our workshop organizer, who has already formed countless workshops as well as five schools of the method.

Further, I would like to extend my humble gratitude to the White Light Expansion instructors. Whenever you connect people who come to you with the subtle layers of consciousness, I am almost certain that something at the depths of the universe quivers with excited response!

From the deepest part of my being, I express gratitude to the spiritual teacher Gabriel Cousens M.D., whose intense studies, both in the field of medicine and in the field of Yoga, have allowed me to profoundly comprehend the human's subtle anatomy, thus establishing the solid philosophical groundwork for this method. In this context, I would like to mention, yet again, the sources of inspiration that supported this method's development: the *Zero Point Process, The Journey, The Work, Past Life Regression,* and *Krishnamurti.* Undoubtedly, without my continuous dialogue with these sources, the White Light Expansion could never have taken root.

And to all of you who read this book, I am grateful for your receptive spirit, which is willing to go as far as to meet one another in the subtlest spaces of the one and only universal mind.

—Shai Tubali

Shai Tubali

A Word to the Reader

- *The instructions in this book do not substitute for medical or psychological care. Whoever chooses to apply the techniques presented throughout the book does so out of his or her own responsibility.*

- *The identities of the people who have generously agreed to share their experiences in the White Light Expansion method have been changed in order to respect their privacy.*

1

Your First Step into Expansion

Everything in this universe is a structure. Every phenomenon in this universe has frontiers and sidewalls, particular shapes, characteristics, and attributes. This does not apply only to visible forms—everyone knows that an African elephant possesses a shape, a color, a character, and a repetitive pattern of behavior—but also to subtler phenomena, such as thoughts, emotions, and sensations, as well as ideas, beliefs, symbols, and human patterns of behavior. In fact, even the universe has a structure, which we can reflect through our consciousness, and indeed, even our consciousness itself has a structure.

The discovery that everything has a structure, and therefore, that everything has a limit, is of crucial importance and goes far beyond mere philosophical implications. Actually, the moment one identifies a structure and its limitations, one can easily transcend it; discovering that which lies beyond limits implies the ability to break through boundaries and to become much broader and freer than the distinct structure itself.

In popular language, it is common to tell a person who is too fixated on a certain pattern of thinking to "Think outside of the box!" Well, this is exactly what we are doing here together. The purpose of this book is to break through limitations, yours and mine. Together, we shall learn to identify structures and then to move beyond their limitations. Whenever we break through a limit, it will become clear to us that we have been somewhat transformed, that we have undergone a tremendous change in our consciousness, thoughts, emotions and feelings. Thus, we will realize that we can be much more than we have ever thought or even imagined possible.

Commonly, the way we use the capacities of our consciousness is pretty narrow: accumulating memory, storing information and knowledge, interpreting on the basis of memory and knowledge, espousing ideas, having uncontrolled dreams, and less commonly, engaging in creative activity through the power of our imagination and subconscious or delving into a scientific inquiry that takes advantage of our capacity for objective thinking. Nevertheless, the truth is that our consciousness bears an enormous, if not inconceivable, scope of flexible directions and motions, and we can delve into it for an entire lifetime and still remain unfulfilled. Just like outer space with its billions of galaxies, which astounds us in its countless possible discoveries, so, too, our consciousness holds within itself a tremendous range of possible experiences, insights, and subtle dimensions.

Some portion of this range has been unveiled by the numerous people throughout human history who have exhausted the potential of meditation and spiritual contemplation. Yet another portion, a quite impressive one, can now be revealed through a highly useful tool of consciousness, which I call "expansion." The expansion is a tool for ecstatic navigation throughout the depths of consciousness.

To be able to carry out an expansion, we actually need very little: only the power of our consciousness and its hidden senses, which are really not so hidden, as we will soon realize. The expansion enables a breakthrough of limitations, and this breakthrough of limitations enables a revelation of the dormant potential that lies at the heart of whatever we might focus our consciousness on.

So, let us begin now. We will focus our consciousness on one object and then carry out an expansion. We will break through limits and realize new possibilities/ways of experiencing and feeling.

We shall begin with a very simple expansion, the expansion of a positive emotion. Of course, we are not used to expanding positive emotions as they seem to be more than enough on their own. The very suggestion indicates that there is something beyond a positive emotion's borders that we ought to find. Why would we expect this? After all, if it were up to us, we would rather abide in positivity as much as possible before sorrowfully collapsing into some negative emotion, pain or even the daily existential tension that follows too many of us! Well, the thing is that, in actuality, positive emotions in their expanded states can lead us to truly sublime experiences, over-flowing bliss, and an existence beyond sorrow, *beyond the ability to suffer*. Simple positive emotion is mostly derived from passing cir-cumstances, depending on some experience, person, or temporary state, while its expansion unveils a new potential, a free and happy existence that is not circumstantial, meaning that it is not caused by anything.

In this spirit, close your eyes for a moment and allow your mind to effortlessly summon the brief time or period in your life during which you experienced the most positive emotion you can think of. Perhaps this would be your wedding night or the miracle of your first child's birth; perhaps it would be a moment in which you cracked open some far-reaching scientific mystery or powerfully experi-enced a state of infinite peace while meditating or abiding in nature. Simply close your eyes, let go for a moment and allow your mind to bring to the surface such a wondrous time.

There is no need to forcefully search within your mind. Every memory of profound experience and positive emotion lies dormant within your cells at this very moment. The happy news is that mem-ories of positive experiences, not only traumatic ones, are fully alive within your being. We tend to say, "This trauma haunts me as if it happened yesterday," but we forget that emotional elevation is also accessible to us at this very moment by contacting a positive living memory. Our positive experiences, too, are accumulated within us as layers of living experience, not merely as nostalgia.

The moment you have tapped into such a living memory, get in touch with it sensually, emotionally, and visually. Bring it up before your mind's eye, and, by breathing and focusing, revive it within you. Feel its interior, and move toward its very heart, its very core. Then, try to vocalize it. What does it feel like? Do not analyze the experience and do not interpret it. Just feel it, intimately, and describe what it *feels like.*

For instance, a woman may bring up the memory of the birth of her first born, a moment in which she experienced peaks of emotional and even spiritual elevation. In response to the question, "What does it feel like?"" she might answer: "It's like a total breakthrough of all limitations, like an opening without an end, like life erupting out of me, like a collaboration with the miracle of creation." This is her first characterization of the emotion's structure.

After you have revived the emotions and the wholesome experience of this memory, it is time to reveal its emotional structure as a visual structure in the full sense of the word. How does one reveal a structure? Each one of us is endowed not only with external senses that enable the full perception and characterization of the visible world, but also with inner senses, the senses of consciousness. We use these senses, among other things, in the dream state. Whenever we dream, we are able to touch, taste, smell, hear, and see things and events that do not possess an objective existence. These very senses will be of use to us as we attempt to identify and characterize structures within our consciousness.

The most important thing in this process is to identify where exactly the structure—in this specific case, the emotional structure—appears within our body. Our body is our first anchor. Whatever we may experience, feel, and even know, will exceptionally awaken one central area in our body. Even when we are dealing with a highly spiritual and abstract state, there is still always one area in the body that reacts to this state the most and interacts with it the most. In this sense, it is the body and not the psyche, or the mind, which should be considered our center of experience.

We may locate the structure anywhere in our body: at the tip of our head or in our sex organs; in our upper belly or at the center of our chest; in the palms of our hands or at the base of our spine. For example, the previously discussed woman who got in touch with her memory of labor might have traced her sense of "opening" to what is regarded as the heart, the intangible emotional center that seems to somehow surround the human chest.

Having located its area in the body, we can now turn our inner senses to the task of identifying, now quite easily, the emotion's form or shape. It is always surprising to realize that every emotion has some energic form that exists somewhere within our being. It may be a geometric shape—a rectangle, a circle, a triangle, a pyramid or an ellipse—but it is also possible that it will be a more elusive image, like something that reminds us of an opening flower, the calm waves of a sea, or a spreading fire.

Then, we will identify the color of the emotion's structure, the central feeling or sensation that accompanies the structure, and also, the fragrance that follows the structure—a fragrance that does not necessarily have to be as tangible as "the smell of a rose" but can be, likewise, a more general ambience, such as "the fragrance of love."

Finally, we will select a general name for the entire structure. A "general name" does not necessarily imply the most accurate title but rather the first name that comes up from within us as we focus on the wholesome structure we have just identified. Thus, the happy woman in labor might identify the structure as a pure white flower at the center of her chest, followed by a central feeling of wholeness and completeness and by the fragrance of utmost beauty. The general name, appearing from within in the face of this emotional structure, would be "new life."

At this stage, we are prepared to carry out the first expansion of the emotional structure. It is quite difficult to expand an abstract phenomenon, such as an emotion. However, as soon as a structure is identified and characterized, it is much easier to expand it and, thus, to discover what lies beyond its limits. What is the furthest state to which the structure of "new life" can lead us? What is the full potential of this structure, the potential that will take us far beyond the familiar limitations of some passing emotional experience or other, which is ordinarily doomed to become no more than a fading memory?

The state of expansion is in the "beyond;" it is going beyond that which we believe possible in the limitations of the known and the familiar. As such, it is the vehicle of consciousness that enables us to move lightly from any narrow and limited state toward a much broader state, maybe even a limitless one. The awesome implication of this is that every briefly-glimpsed state of happiness can turn into bliss, and every irritating, negative emotion can become, from one expansion to another, a tool for the total transcendence of our spirit.

We carry out an expansion in the following way: we breathe into the structure and allow it to expand more and more through the power of imagination aided by the power of breath (with time, the structure will expand as a natural impulse of the consciousness without any "doing" on our part). This is where we will use the specific areas in our bodies and the specific shapes or images we have identified. They will be our anchors, our most vivid and tangible reference points, throughout the process of expansion.

Now, the very fact that we have identified the structure implies that our consciousness is far vaster than the structure itself, does it not? What previously seemed gigantic, and perhaps even uncontainable, now seems to be both containable and perceivable within our consciousness. Again, one can only expand that which has clearly characterized frontiers and sidewalls, that which has a beginning, a middle, and an end.

Keep in mind this highly important point. We will need it when we move on to self-therapy and poignant negative emotions. It is naturally easier to identify the limits of a positive emotion, which we are ready and gladly willing to re-experience. It is harder, at least at the beginning, to agree to revive a negative emotion and then to dare to define its frontiers. There are certain negative emotions that seem infinite to us. It feels as if contacting them would inevitably lead us into a bottomless pit of sorrow. Thus, by our very willingness to contain the structure within our consciousness and stay with it without escaping, condemning, justifying, or identifying it, we have already begun to transcend it. We have identified ourselves as a vaster space of awareness, which can allow anything to appear in it without the interference of attraction or repulsion, and as this space, we have simultaneously agreed to let this structure be while at the same time expressing an explicit intention for the sake of our own development to transcend its familiar borders.

So, in this wondrous state where we accept and contain whatever the structure is precisely as it is while at the same time seeking to transcend it, we guide the structure to expand more and more until it reaches its outermost limits, until it cannot expand anymore. We guide it to show itself to us in its entirety. It can be remarkable to realize that the structure indeed obeys such a request, yet this is but a simple first step on the path that leads us to becoming the masters and true owners of our consciousness.

The dynamics of the expansion of a structure can be likened to the increasing inflation of a balloon, which at one point attains its maximum limit and then explodes. In the same way, the structure tries to "show" us, as it were, how far it can reach until it finally bursts and assimilates into a greater space.

Our new mother who recalled her experience of giving birth can now use the power of imagination and feeling to breathe into and expand the white flower in her heart. The flower might grow to the extent that it encompasses the entire body and even outgrows it. It may seem as if her body exists within the flower and not vice versa. However, at some point, the flower will not be able to expand anymore, and then it will be revealed that the structure actually exists within a greater space. In a sense, the flower will be absorbed into this space, and our consciousness will expand to the size of this new plane, which goes beyond the limits of the emotion with which we entered the process in the first place.

"Give a general name to the expanded emotion," we would then ask the woman who is re-experiencing and expanding the moment of her child's birth.

Now that her consciousness is vaster and more wholesome, she might entitle the expanded state "a complete self-wholeness." This "complete self-wholeness" is a greater and broader state than the initial state, called "new life." While the "new life" was a circumstantial emotion, depending on the experience of birth giving, "complete self-wholeness" is more of a quality of being rather than some familiar emotion.

"New life" is a causal emotion; "complete self-wholeness" is a non-causal emotion. You can experience "complete self-wholeness" at any given moment, not only in the midst of an exciting birth. You can experience it while boringly waiting for a bus or a train, while routinely waking up in the morning, or even shortly before closing your eyes and sinking into sleep.

In this way, just as with the well-known Babushka (or Matryoshka) doll, in the process of expanding the initial positive emotion, we pass into ever-greater spaces, while, at every stage, the previous space, which might have seemed vast enough to us, is assimilated into the one that was revealed afterward. As with the Babushka, while the innermost "doll" of the initial emotion is the densest, all other, larger "dolls" are increasingly more hollow and airy.

At each and every stage, we will carry out the expansion process, and, immediately afterward, we will characterize the new structure or plane with a general name for what it feels like, whether it is an area in the body, a shape, an image, a color, a feeling, a sensation, a fragrance or an ambience. Slowly but surely our new mother will be moving from "new life" to "complete self-wholeness," from "complete self-wholeness" to "limitless space," from "limitless space" to "absolute freedom," and from "absolute freedom" to what she might entitle, for lack of more appropriate words, "God" or "Infinity."

On our way along the process of expansion, we will have to overcome a very significant conditioning: we are not used to feeling *that* blissful, *that* great. We are accustomed to being content with very little, with a minuscule amount of joy, and, from time to time, a low or medium voltage of positive emotion. Rarely do we allow ourselves to feel overjoyed, overflowing, and bursting with bliss or love or inner conviction and wholeness. This is partly because our cynical environment does not tend to support such "naïve" feelings, not to mention that these feelings serve as disturbing reflections of the compromises that others around us make in their own lives. But it is also so because life has taught us that shortly after a positive experience, there awaits us, just around the corner, an emotional pain or some sort of physical suffering—life turns upside down, and we, who acutely depend on its ups and downs, might undergo a terribly disillusioning fall back into the ordinary and the known.

There is yet another reason: social morality has instilled in us a wariness of the life force bubbling within us. It warns us that when the life force overflows, it might drive us to act in unbridled ways, and we will "get burned." We learned in childhood to minimize our experiences so that no one would get hurt, especially not us.

Hence the conditioning: we must not be too happy. But how far in our lives has this obedience to the law brought us, really? The experiment has failed, and we, being part of this wondrous life, deserve more, so much more.

It is possible that along the process of expansion, as our being expands toward this state of sublime bliss, negative emotions or physical tensions of all sorts will all of a sudden appear, attempting, as it were, to distract us from the expanded planes. In reality, these tensions are not to be regarded as "enemies" of the expanded planes, and we, therefore, should not perceive their presence as an evidence of a sudden "falling from grace." On the contrary, their appearance assures us that a process of purification and liberation is taking place in the body-mind complex. As our being expands, a new energy is released and starts flowing within us; just like an excited and ecstatic river, it stumbles upon the dens we ourselves have constructed by clinging to erroneous beliefs, thoughts, and emotions. The solution is simple indeed: just turn your attention to the space itself, characterize it as a structure, and then keep on expanding. At one moment, the all-inclusive harmony, which is typical of these planes, will flow into your body and mind and transform them into harmonious, healthy and blissful systems. Start the change within your being, and the body and mind will follow it shortly after.

Keep expanding. Perform about five expansions. It is very likely that after two or three you will feel that you are no longer capable of expanding—try to push it just a little further. Nonetheless, at a certain point, you will reach a state that you will feel is not expandable. That means that, as far as you know at this stage of your evolution, this state has no limits. Thus, you have reached a state of no-limitation. This state is more precious than gold and the key to infinite possibilities, which will be discussed in this book.

Remember: whenever you carry out the process of expansion, the states of consciousness that you reach will always be far more developed and greater than your previous attainments. The reason is that the process of expansion makes your consciousness expand in the fullest sense of the word so whatever struck you as limitless at one point will simply become the first expanded plane that you will easily reach next time.

In this way, you are encountering your true being. The positive emotion transforms into a gateway through which you can pass into the infinite planes of your consciousness. Slowly but surely, you become less and less dependent on circumstances, people, and passing experiences, and you get to meet the most profound emotions, in their purest state, within your own self. This is true freedom.

Through the process of expansion, you begin to contact enlightened feelings and emotions. Some practitioners attain, at one stage or another, a state called, "The White Light" (a state whose essence and significance will be explained in the next chapter; it is not a coincidence that this is the name of the entire system): their consciousness is flooded with the glittering light of their spiritual being. But, beyond the White Light plane, there are other enormous planes waiting to be explored and fully experienced by us.

In quite a short while, you will be able to experience states that, in the past, one could only experience through an effortful and consistent meditation practice that persevered for months or even years. This is possible because the White Light expansion is the fastest, most direct, and most conscious way to expand consciousness.

Welcome to the world of expansion! Let us begin!

Practice: The Expansion of Positive Emotions

Expanding a positive emotion can be a wonderful way to start your day. However, it can be performed in almost any situation and at almost all times. As emphasized in the introduction, it is highly recommended to try out expansion, at least in your first attempts, with a friend guiding you.

Important: whenever you see this mark, "..." it is your sign to pause for a few seconds in order to either receive a response or settle into and deepen a new state.

1. Sit in a comfortable position and close your eyes. Allow your entire being to relax more and more. Breathe slowly and deeply... You are about to enter into your innermost Self... to enjoy a state of self-knowing, which is the sweetest and most wondrous state possible... Now, from this relaxation, let the moment or time in your life in which you experienced the highest level of happiness, elevation, and limitlessness rise to the surface of your mind. Recall the situation within yourself. Where are you? ... What are your feelings? ... What are your physical sensations? ... Give a general name to the general feeling... Look for the area in your body in which the general feeling appears the most...

2. Get in touch with the general feeling. First, feel it as it appears in the situation... and then let go of the situation and remain only with the general feeling. Breathe into it. Feel it deeply while using the specific area in the body in which it is felt the most... Again, let the situation come up, and feel the general feeling as it appears within it... Then, remove the situation and remain only with the feeling. Breathe into it... For the last time: let the situation appear in your mind, feel the general feeling within it... and then remove the situation completely and remain only with the feeling...

3. Breathe into the general feeling. Move into its depth, into its very core. Try to describe it with words. What does it feel like? ... Look for an area in the body that is deeply connected to it... a shape or an image... a color... a general sensation... a fragrance...

4. Feel this general feeling from within. Breathe into it. Allow it to spread wider and deeper. Let it fill your entire body and being. Breathe into the image or shape in the area of the body that you have located, and let it continue to expand until it reaches its outermost limit, until it cannot expand anymore. Request: "General Feeling, show yourself completely to me!" ...

5. Give a name to the expanded state... Breathe into the expanded state. Move into its depth, into its very core. Try to describe it in words. What does it feel like? ...

6. Look closely. Who are you in this state? ... How do you understand the meaning and purpose of life from this state? ... Abide in this state. Sense and feel it from within... Allow your body-mind complex to re-charge in this sublime state... Look for an area in the body that is deeply connected to this state... a shape or an image... a color... a general sensation... a fragrance...

7. Feel this expanded state from within. Breathe into it. Allow it to spread wider and deeper. Let it fill your entire body and being. Breathe into the image or shape in the area of the body that you have located, and let it expand more and more until it reaches its outermost limit, until it cannot expand anymore. Request: "Expanded State, show yourself completely to me!" ...

8. Give a name to the expanded state... Breathe into the expanded state. Move into its depth, into its very core. Try to describe it in words. What does it feel like? ...

9. Look closely. Who are you in this state? ... How do you understand the meaning and purpose of life from this state? ... Abide in this state. Sense and feel it from within... Allow your body-mind complex to re-charge in this sublime state... Look for an area in the body that is deeply connected to this state... a shape or an image... a color... a general sensation... a fragrance...

10. Feel this expanded state from within. Breathe into it. Allow it to spread wider and deeper. Let it fill your entire body and being. Breathe into the image or shape in the area of the body that you have located, and let it expand more and more until it reaches its outermost limit, until it cannot expand anymore. Request: "Expanded state, show yourself completely to me!" ...

11. Give a name to the expanded state... Breathe into the expanded state. Move into its depth, into its very core. Try to describe it in words. What does it feel like? ...

12. Look closely. Who are you in this state? ... How do you understand the meaning and purpose of life from this state? ... Abide in this state. Sense and feel it from within... Allow your body-mind complex to re-charge in this sublime state... Look for an area in the body that is deeply connected to this state... a shape or an image... a color... a general sensation... and a fragrance...

13. Feel this expanded state from within. Breathe into it. Allow it to spread wider and deeper. Let it fill your entire body and being. Breathe into the image or shape in the area of the body that you have located, and let it expand more and more until it reaches its outermost limit, until it cannot expand anymore. Request: "Expanded State, show yourself completely to me!" ...

14. Finally, encode the body-mind complex to align with the most expanded state... You have learned that positive emotions are a gateway to the divine reality that is hidden deep within you. Positive emotions can be expanded toward infinity... Can you now see, from the beginning of the process, the potential for expansion of this general feeling? ... Express gratitude toward the initial feeling that lead you into this most expanded state...

15. For the last time, immerse yourself in this expanded state for self-remembrance and liberation... Remember: who you really are transcends all emotions, and this

transcendence is true meditation. Before you open your eyes, choose to keep in contact with this state within your heart, even in your ordinary state of consciousness. Now you may gently open your eyes.

A sharing

S., 20 years old, completely inexperienced in spiritual practices and in therapeutic processes, after her first experience expanding a positive emotion.

When I was asked, at the beginning of the process, to revive the most positive experience in my life, the first image that came into my mind was the day on which I had parachuted for the first time. I had been waiting to jump from the tiny plane; my entire body was already outside of it, and I had felt sure of myself—happy, free and limitless. I had felt that it would be much better to be up in the sky than down on the ground. When I took the leap, it was like floating, and my entire body felt fresh and alive. I was particularly excited while hovering over the sea and seeing the green areas all around.

I identified the emotion as "Freedom" and located it in my heart. It felt like confidence and also, lightness, as if all my cells were opening up. The shape was a circle; the color, pink; the feeling, lightheartedness; and the fragrance, rosy.

In the first expansion, I reached the plane of "Love," a good feeling, hot, as if warm water was showering down on my entire body. The plane was centered in my head; the image was of transparent water; the feeling was warm, and the fragrance rosy.

In this plane, I realized that positive emotions were meant to lead us to happiness, to empower us, to make us love ourselves, and also, to enable us to love the world. The positive emotion bestowed freedom on me, making me a bird that is free to fly. I discovered that, on this plane, I'm a good person, that the meaning and purpose of life is to attain a full realization of goodness, and also, that we're here to protect animals, the entire world, and the world's inherent goodness.

In the second expansion, I reached the plane of "Stillness." The plane felt like a place of calmness as if I were sitting on a small rock and resting in the midst of a stream. The plane filled my whole body. The image was of a tree; the sensation was "treeness;" and the fragrance was "tree-like."

I felt as if I were a tiny seed. Here, I realized that the meaning of life is love and understanding. In regard to my sleeping disorders, I understood that fear was what made it hard for me to sleep. I was afraid to sleep because I didn't want to dream, and I was also afraid of waking up in the morning because I didn't want to cope with the world. I saw that I could actually stop this habit of fear and that life is a game. I can play around with it. I can start doing things for myself, whatever comes to me at any given moment—create, work, or go to the sea.

In the third expansion, I reached the plane of "Infinity." In this state, I realized that I am light. I understood that the meaning of life is to love oneself and accept the world. I saw that the fear of sleep is foolish as there is nothing to be afraid of. I discovered that I could close my eyes without having to think of anything if I wanted to. I simply had to connect with the infinite stillness and, from there, naturally sink into sleep.

I saw that I am actually very strong. Nothing could ever break me. Only I can break myself. I could, however, identify with the wrong thoughts and thus create the illusion of a broken self. Therefore, I discovered that I should disconnect myself from all emotions and doubts—simply disconnect!

After opening my eyes, an inner message remained with me: I'm really unbreakable. Nothing could ever break me again.

2

The Secret of Expansion

What Actually Is an Expansion?

Before we unveil the basic principle behind the process of expansion, let us take a straightforward look at our present experience of life. If we closely examine the consistent characteristics of all our psychological and physiological struggles and blockages, we will soon realize that the most common element underlying them all is, first and foremost, a feeling of contraction. Another possible way to describe this feeling could be limitation or suffocation. On even deeper inspection, we will discover that the experience of suffering and distress is *caused* by the feeling of contraction. Tension and stress, fear and disappointment, and obsessive thoughts and stomachaches are all characterized by contractions. It is as if something is not properly flowing and not "breathing" well. It is as if something is moving in a narrow and annoying groove, "closing in" on our mind and oppressing it.

In stark contrast, the constant characteristic of wellbeing and health is the feeling of expansion, or the breakthrough of limitations. Out of density and a sense of being "stuck," something all at once opens up, and we experience more airiness, flow, and breathing space. On the physical plane, sickness and pain are states of contraction, excess, and congestion, whereas health is a natural and flowing movement of fluids, blood, and oxygen. Tension is a physical contraction, and relaxation is its expansion. On the emotional plane, fear (as only one example) is the narrowing down of our entire being into a single emotion, whereas happiness is just the opposite—making us feel that we have no limitations whatsoever.

Thus, if we wakefully observe the general feeling that characterizes suffering in comparison to the general feeling that characterizes happiness, joy and health, our final conclusion will be quite obvious:

- The feeling of limitation and contraction *is* suffering.

- The feeling of expansion and limitlessness *is* bliss.

For the most part, our daily experience is one of constant existential tension, conscious and unconscious. Nowadays, it is quite clear to all that human suffering is not caused merely by natural disasters and the reality of aging and dying. In fact, human suffering is caused *mainly* by ideas, emotions, and thoughts that are the handiwork of the human itself. The most crucial suffering that a human being will undergo in a lifetime is not derived from life itself but from the world that mankind has created through ideas and emotions. It is all interconnected: the terrible famine in Africa is the outcome of the unfair distribution of the earth's resources, and this unfair distribution is the outcome of the order created by human consciousness. Obsessive thinking and self-destructive behavior are inseparably related to our overwhelmingly stressful way of life, our artificial nutrition, and our total ignorance concerning knowledge that might instill peace and contentment in our consciousness. Our prime defect stems from within our consciousness—or, to be more precise, from the fact that our consciousness is far too contracted.

Generally, our self-experience is one of contraction and limitation. Our mental world moves mostly in tiny, closed, and repetitive circles, which tend to bring about self-destruction. Our emotional world is too often a sort of prison from which we do not know how to escape, and our ability to find creative solutions that might lead us away from our captivity is limited. For the most part, our mind's attention is focused on the surface of existence, on daily worries and irritations, on wants and needs (the real ones as well as the many false ones), on fears and desires and on the countless "problems" of the body and psyche. We hardly get to know the awesome feeling of our consciousness when it is in its expanded, unworried state, liberated from all tension and irritation. In the absence of the ability to evoke this feeling by ourselves, we tend to be attracted to temporary distractions and pleasures, which are nothing but cheap substitutes for the expansion of consciousness.

As pointed out earlier, contraction is suffering, and expansion is bliss. Now, we shall add a highly important principle to our equation: the contraction of consciousness is suffering, while the expansion of consciousness is bliss. If so, it is very likely that the expansion of consciousness is the key to easing human suffering, both inner and outer, the key to liberating ourselves from our destructive psychological structure, as well as the key to finding new creative solutions to the world's greatest distresses. After all, it is the contracted consciousness that created these problems in the first place! Contraction creates the sickness, and therefore expansion can bring about true and everlasting health.

At the beginning of this book, we learned how to carry out the expansion of a positive emotion. You might have been surprised to realize that a positive emotion is a structure that should be broken through. For the expanded consciousness, any kind of fixed structure—any pattern that repeats itself over and over again—is a form of suffering since structure implies contraction. Moving out of a structure into a new plane always implies an increase of bliss, joy, and elevation, and hence, an increase of creativity, life force, and intelligence.

Fortunately, the urge to expand and to remove limitations exists within the consciousness of each of us. We do not need to invent it. This urge "knows" that the establishment of limitations is followed by a feeling of suffocation and discomfort in stark contrast to the breaking through of limitations, which is followed by a tremendous sense of relief. We often seek to shatter limitations through child-ish rebellions against social conventions. We attempt to feel free by disobeying social orders, but in doing so, we miss the fact that libera-tion from limitations must, before anything else, take place within the consciousness. The distress is an inner distress, and therefore, the solution must take place deep within.

The process of expansion is, fundamentally, the process of in-creasing internal bliss. It grants the consciousness the capacity to overcome its own barriers and overpower the contracted state in which it has been imprisoned. The expansion is the power that en-ables us to overcome any blockage in our consciousness, such as repetitive and circular thought patterns. Before anything else, it enables this by quickly turning whatever appears to be too big to handle into amazingly tiny components compared to the conscious-ness itself. The consciousness expands far beyond the limitations of emotional and mental patterns and thus overpowers its barriers and moves into a freer and more limitless state.

At the same time, the expansion is also an alchemical process: it transmutes every cheap metal (emotion, thought, feeling, idea, or problem) into gold as it reveals the utmost and ultimate poten-tial—the *spirituality,* if you would like—of every energy within us. Through its power, every element in us becomes more conscious and wholesome, more liberated and expanded. It catalyzes, unleash-es, and accelerates every blockage and hindrance. It does not allow anything to stagnate. It drives everything toward liberation from "gravity" and raises everything to the limitless skies.

In other words, the expansion is the passage:
- from the contracted to the expanded;
- from the dense to the airy;
- from the hard to the lighthearted;
- from the limited to the unlimited;
- from the impossible to the possible;
- from the structure to the breakthrough of the structure;
- from the causal to the non-causal;

- from the conditioned to the unconditioned; and

- from the material to the spiritual.

Let us say, for example, that I have an acute headache. A headache is, of course, a state of contraction, compression, excess, and congestion. As soon as I perform an expansion on the headache, it will transform into the emotional state or the mental burden that brought it about in the first place, that is, it will transform into a subtler energy. With another expansion, the emotional state or the mental burden will be transformed (or, more precisely, expanded since transmutation in our context is expansion), and the very feeling of contraction, which entraps our head in a terrible pain, will be replaced with a new flow. Abiding in this expanded state of consciousness, the head will "breathe anew," and the energy within it will begin to flow properly and unrestrained. Even if we need to perform four, five, or six expansions to reach that state, the feeling of actual liberation will be worthwhile: the contraction may turn, through this alchemical act, into an expansion, and we will very likely be able to enjoy the desired sense of health with an additional side effect, the bliss of consciousness, which no painkiller can ever provide for us!

Expansion and the Creation of the World

Let us now "expand" the context in which the principle of expansion is activated. In the teachings of Ha'Ari (Isaac Luria, 1534-1572), which to this day are considered the prime interpretations of the Kabala, the process of creation is presented as a process of contraction. The infinite divine light contracted itself, more and more, into structures, and this is, in fact, the created world as we know it: a denser, or more contracted, divine light. Matter is, in effect, a condensed or contracted spirit.

From this astounding point of view, we can perceive the entire universe as narrow channels through which divine energy flows, as formations containing a condensed divine light. Each form and every structure are nothing but an "entrapped" light, a light that was limited so as to create and make visible the form or the structure.

Hence, contraction was a necessity in the original divine creation. Without it, creation could not have existed at all.

Since the process of creation is an ever increasing contraction, the human consciousness pays quite a price for it: somewhere in the far end of the chain of contraction, man encounters his frightening smallness and the numerous limitations of his consciousness, psyche, and body. Trapped in the narrow body and the countless trivial details of daily life, he experiences a fundamental suffering, which is primarily unconscious. This suffering is the nagging and troubling knowledge that, deep inside, he is nothing but an "entrapped" divine light. The nature of this light is unlimited and infinite space, just as it was before the contracting process of the creation of the universe. The implication is that only when a human directly contacts this unlimited nature will he succeed in experiencing an essential happiness *while still* residing in the contracted structure of the body-mind complex.

One could say that this is the most profound motivation for man's yearning for freedom: the urge to break through the structure in which he is trapped since, unlike other biological creatures on this planet, he recognizes through his awareness his own fullest potential, his own ability to break free from the structure. But how can man, being placed in such a contracted structure, be as wide as the illuminated infinity?

Throughout the ages, different techniques have appeared, aiming to provide the human being with the liberating experience of the expanded state: meditation, mantras, prayer, and more. Each technique has actually been an unconscious form of expansion—unconscious since man has not referred to it this way and has not necessarily known the one and only purpose of his practices. Due to this lack of awareness, too often his mind has been distracted and shifted to a more limited kind of spirituality, focusing on symbols, ideas, beliefs, and objects of worship. Man has not realized that the one thing he has attempted to achieve through all of these practices is the expansion of his consciousness.

In actuality, genuine spirituality *is* an expansion of our consciousness. One can certainly go as far as to claim that this expansion is the opposite of contraction, of divine creation: if, before, the divine light had contracted more and more until it manifested, at the end of this process we began to expand our tiny and limited brain toward infinity. In this context, the meaning and purpose of life is to expand out of the limited until the limited becomes the unlimited. The purpose is not to return to the source, as some teachings suggest. It is not about contracting back into the state of pre-creation; the intention is the very opposite: to evolve, to outgrow the structures, and to burst out of them so that the universe itself becomes divine. In other words, the journey is from expansion to contraction and from contraction to expansion. The new expansion is the continuation of creation through humans. The purpose of this journey of life is not to go back, but it is also not exactly about moving forward. Development means expansion: spreading out from the center, from the core, just like the continuously unfolding cosmos.

Through the extremely simple process of expansion, we can finally directly do what the human being indirectly attempted to do for ages. Now, we can be an expanded consciousness from within the body without any need for religious custom and convention. An expanded consciousness, which is our natural measure, knows what is right for itself and so is capable of being an authority unto itself and creating through its own power.

Moreover, an expanded consciousness is capable of performing the magic of alchemy: through the act of expansion, it can transform any matter into spirit, extricating the broadest, fullest, and optimal potential of each and every element in this universe. It is capable of unleashing the trapped divine light and then expanding it to its most complete realization.

Expansion Is All We Need

Expansion is all we need for a happy and complete existence within the physical body. For that purpose, my aim in this book is to enable you to turn the act of expansion into a habit, into second nature. As soon as you get used to expanding everything all the time, the expanded consciousness will start to become your very own permanent state. The process of expansion will allow you, again and again, to overcome the "force of gravity" or, more precisely, the force of contraction: a new energy will flow in your body and brain, your consciousness will become bright and liberated, blissful emotions will sprout from your depths, and wisdom and inner knowledge will start to blossom until this activity may become who you are. It will become your very being. Instead of "doing" expansions, your consciousness will expand as if by itself, without any special effort on your part. At a certain stage, it will be able to attain the final, ultimate expansion, the one that many regard as "Enlightenment." Put simply, Enlightenment is the state in which consciousness expands until its boundaries shatter and it is absorbed into a greater space, the space of cosmic or divine consciousness. Just like with our previously discussed positive emotion, which reaches its outermost limits and then assimilates into a new state, so, too, our individual contracted consciousness will outgrow its own self-structure and merge with the uncontracted and unlimited space. In this state, there is absolute self-knowledge, absolute certainty, and absolute bliss.

Through the White Light Expansion, you may freely experience the awakened state and even apply it to problem-solving, creativity, healing and self-empowerment. Yet, beyond one experience or another, a deeper attraction to the state itself might be aroused within you, a state increasingly more achievable as we turn the expansion process into a habit, into a moment-to-moment inner activity.

The Theory of Subtle Fields

Without profound insight into the structure of consciousness, it would be impossible to adequately comprehend the White Light method and the expansion process in particular. Of course, one can carry out the act of expansion very successfully even without such an understanding, but the additional level of awareness may turn this powerful and elusive experience into a more sensible and meaningful realization. As the title of this chapter betrays, the Theory of Subtle Fields (see Diagram A at the back of this book) can endow us with the explanation for how, systematically and routinely, hundreds of thousands of people have reached the same states of consciousness through the White Light method. Obviously, in the absence of a suitable scientific instrument at this stage of human evolution, this is but a theory, which can be validated through direct experience alone. Nevertheless, it is capable of answering many important questions concerning the method.

The Theory of Subtle Fields is, in many respects, the only plausible explanation for the interaction between the physical brain and the dimensions of the mind and spirituality, dimensions which are partly a daily experience for all humans and partly the shared experience of a minute percentage of the world population along the ages. It provides us with the highly needed bridge between the visible and the invisible. This theory is not a lone voice in the wilderness. It has many parallels in various traditions and acclaimed spiritual teachings (among others, one can mention the teachings of the Yogic tradition, the Theosophical Society, Rudolf Steiner, and Osho). These doctrines explicitly suggest that man does not own solely a physical body but rather several bodies (or fields) that encompass a physical body. Some have suggested a division into four bodies, some five or six, and a few even went as far as suggesting seven; despite the numerical differences, the essential division is always the same. One way or another, these bodies are the bearers of the developmental and spiritual potential of man. Without them, man's consciousness cannot expand beyond its known borders. Moreover, these bodies, or fields, are the explanation for the countless accounts of the human experiences in all traditions, religions, and philosophies of states of consciousness beyond or outside the brain.

The Electromagnetic Field

The first field, which in our theory is called the *"the electromagnetic field,"* is the energic structure that envelops the body, and therefore, exists in close proximity to it. This field is the closest, in essence, to the physical plane. Every human body is surrounded by such a field. Planet earth itself is enveloped by an inclusive electromagnetic field, and, naturally, interconnections exist between the individual electromagnetic fields and the inclusive field of the earth. Through the electromagnetic field, we interact with other fields of the physical plane, and, accordingly, this field is quite vulnerable and susceptible to environmental influences of all sorts: from collective human influences, to the influences of animals, to the effects of the electromagnetic field of the planet, and even to the fields of other planets.

Being the energic equivalent of the physical body, this field possesses its own anatomy. Nowadays, everyone knows the term *chakra*, the name for the seven primary centers of energy that operate within the electromagnetic field. In the Yogic tradition, these energy centers are actually seven conjunction points between the 72,000 nadis that constitute man's energic nervous system. The most fundamental role of the chakras is to magnetize the energic nourishment, which flows from the subtler planes of existence toward them and to translate this nourishment into a life-sustaining force for the sake of the physical body. Each and every chakra, according to its location in the body, attracts the cosmic life force and translates it into an available energy for the glands, organs, and nervous networks that reside in its surroundings. This energy is the "breath of life," the generating power that fills our physical bodies with the "warm" presence of life. This energy is known as *Chi* in traditions such as Chinese medicine and Taoism, and as *Prana* (the cosmic life force) in the Ayurvedic (Hindu medicine) and Yogic traditions. Additionally, each chakra is connected to specific mental, emotional, and sensual impressions, which are accumulated within them and hinder the optimal flow of the life force.

It is quite easy to get directly in touch with the chakras. Through the process of expansion and through many other methods, it is possible to experience the subtle streams of life force, which seem to somehow follow the body and encompass it but not really exist in it. Moreover, each one of us intuitively identifies the chakras, by the sheer fact that we point at the center of our chests as if it were the location of our sense of selfhood or, alternatively, of our "broken heart" and we all readily say that it is not wise to keep our emotions stuck in the "belly." Thus, the most immediate contact that humans can make with the invisible plane of the subtle fields is through the chakras.

Since every field is seen as a dormant potential, the potential that lies within the electromagnetic field would be the awakening of an entire subtle anatomy. The more we expand our consciousness, the more the energy of the life force (the *Kundalini*), which is coiled at the base of the energic spine, begins to awaken and to climb its way upward, breaking through mental, emotional, and sensual blockages in the chakras and unifying the chakras along one central column, which in the Yogic tradition is called the *Sushumna nadi* (the prime energic nervous conductor). The Sushumna conducts the life force in an atypical, reversed flow. Ordinarily, the life force moves in accordance with the force of gravity, that is, downward, toward our earthly, survival-oriented being, but along with its increasing flow in the Sushumna, the life force begins to rise upward, toward the brain and the tip of the head. When it reaches the brain and the tip of the head, it literally floods them with new energy. Eventually, the surge in the energic spine breaks through the tip of the head to the degree that pure cosmic energy starts to descend from the crown of the head along the Sushumna. This cosmic energy progressively turns the entire being of the human into an increasingly spiritual and "divine" entity.

In sum, the electromagnetic field is crucial, as it is our energic body that dramatically influences the flow of life force within our physical body. In addition, the moment our energic body is awake and active, it is possible to increasingly interact with the other, subtler fields. This field becomes easily accessible both for direct experience and for development through the vast range of White Light techniques.

The Mental-Emotional Field

The second field, called the *"mental-emotional field,"* carries within it the reservoir of mental and emotional impressions and imprints, individual and collective alike. It can also be said that this field carries within it not only our conscious impressions, but also, primarily, our unconscious impressions (that is, the personal and collective "subconscious").

According to the Theory of Subtle Fields, all environmental data are registered in the brain but undergo a process of interpretation and categorization in accordance with the impressions and imprints found in the mental-emotional field. In other words, this field molds the brain's pathways of psychological interpretation, and it makes us experience things in one particular way. It seems that when we arrived in this world, we did not come as *tabula rasa* but rather as established psychological beings with predetermined forms of thinking. In my mind, it is very hard to explain the fixed structures with which we all arrived in this world merely by means of genetics and environmental influences. It is likely that our deepest impressions, which many relate to reincarnation, are accumulated in the second field and, from there, activate the brain.

One may posit that the connection between the mental-emotional field and the brain is two-way: as the brain picks new impressions and imprints, they are gathered eventually (perhaps even after physical death) into the field, and, simultaneously, impressions and imprints existing in this field shape the brain in the first place.

This field is of crucial importance in the White Light method since its purification of impressions and imprints and of beliefs and patterns, can dramatically liberate the brain and the entire body from emotional and mental influences that inhibit our freedom and patterns of behavior as well as the choices we make in this life. In fact, all of the therapeutic activity of the White Light focuses on the liberation of the second field, and this liberation is made possible through a principle that we will extensively explore throughout this book: one can influence each field from the subtler field just above it.

The Mental-Spiritual Field

The third field, entitled the *"mental-spiritual field,"* is the first spiritual plane. As the name suggests, this is the field in which the subtlest and airiest thought, stemming from our spiritual being, exists. In this field, one can find spiritual insights, intuitions, visions, mystical symbols, angelic entities, and messages from "above." We can experience spiritual love and profound, non-causal positive emotions (that is, non-circumstantial emotions), feel ourselves more as "souls" and less as bodies and minds in time and space, and get in touch with feelings of eternity, self-expansion, fundamental certainty, and a general sense of freedom.

Real channelers are, possibly, the ones who know how to align their mental-spiritual field with the mental-spiritual field of different forces or entities. Psychoactive plants and psychedelic drugs are unbridled ways to contact this field. Another example is a near-death experience, in which the person all at once becomes conscious of his own spiritual being as it is steeped in the light and as such becomes free from fear, directly knowing what love is. In effect, many of those who report that they have undergone a "spiritual awakening" were endowed with a short-term or a long-term glimpse into the third field.

This field, too, is of considerable importance to the White Light method since, through it, one can greatly influence the less expanded and far more problematic field: the mental-emotional field. In the third field, we are all at once liberated from any sense of problem and conflict; life no longer seems like a merciless process of unbearable challenges but rather a spiritual journey from which one could extricate marvelous learning if only one stopped fearing it so much. Without the sense of problem and existential tension and without the desperate need for affirmation and love, everything suddenly seems possible.

The Cosmic-Soul Field

The fourth field, called the *"cosmic-soul field,"* is a deeper spiritual plane, in which divine or cosmic intelligence becomes accessible. It is what can be thought of as "God's brain" (the brain that Einstein desired with all his might to crack). The, so to speak, "master plan" of the entire cosmos resides in the fourth field along with its most fundamental laws and principles and the hidden logic which binds it all. There one can discover the divine will, directly contact the meaning and purpose of life and in general, study life objectively and trans-personally. In the same breath, one can reveal the nature of the souls' journey along with its laws of development and its different hierarchical structures. Tremendous traditions of wisdom, such as Kabala and Yoga, derive their insights from this field.

The experience in this field may be one of a divine self that possesses a unique aspect (or, in other words, a soul). The individual identifies himself as a divine spark whose nature is eternal and who is, essentially, united with the greater and wholesome divinity.

The Field of Pure Awareness

The fifth field, entitled the *"field of pure awareness,"* is the most spiritual plane, in which we can contact the inconceivable meditative states of unity, pure consciousness, limitlessness, infinite consciousness, God consciousness, or any other word or phrase we might choose. Often, in this plane, the sense of reality is so absolute that we find ourselves depicting it as "infinite space" or even as "absolute nothingness" as it is a state beyond perception and any form of duality. The fifth field, as one may very well guess, is the one in which we can get in touch with what Gautama the Buddha named *Nirvana*, the Hindus called *Brahman*, and different spiritual masters regarded as "the consciousness of infinity" and "absolute reality."

Both the fourth and the fifth fields are accessible for us through the White Light and are exposable at any stage in our expanding process according to the level of our receptivity and willingness.

Other Sources on the Existence of Encompassing Fields

We previously mentioned other sources which had testified, by means of direct experience and self-research, to the existence of fields or bodies that encompass the physical body. Now, we can easily identify parallels between the five fields and the documentation of these sources.

In the Yogic world, four bodies are delineated: physical, subtle, causal, and non-causal.

H.P. Blavatsky, founder of the Theosophical Society, suggested seven bodies, including the physical body, astral, pranic, will, egoic, soul and true-self. The astral, pranic and will correspond to our first field, while the other three are quite aligned with the three spiritual fields.

The 20th century spiritual teacher Osho also spoke of seven bodies: emotional, etheric, astral, mental, spiritual, cosmic, and nirvanic. In this case, too, the analogy is quite precise, particularly in the case of the three subtlest fields. Similarly, the Yogic healer Gabriel

Cousens suggests seven bodies, which are, in his words, "subtle layers of energy and consciousness surrounding the physical body:" etheric, emotional, mental, astral, spiritual, causal and soul. Osho and Cousens alike posit that each one of the seven bodies interacts with its parallel chakra.

Of special interest to us is the analogy between the Theory of Subtle Fields and the theory of the six koshas (*kosha*, in Sanskrit, means *layer*) developed by the 20th century Hindu spiritual teacher Anandamurti. This classification into six layers of consciousness, which in many respects is derived from the Hindu Vedas scriptures, starts with the "food body" (or physical body), and moves on to the desire body (or "pranic" body, the equivalent of the electromagnetic field), the mental-emotional body, the supramental body, the causal body, and the bliss body.

According to Anandamurti, the fourth layer—the supramental body, which is the perfect equivalent of the third, mental-spiritual field—is a natural, spontaneous, and illuminated state, in which we begin to liberate ourselves from the bondage of time, space, and existence, and experience deep peace and spiritual silence. In this state, various abilities, such as intuition, creative insight, and seeing into the past, present, and future appear and develop. Throughout human history, the unique individuals who gave birth to inventions and discoveries in art and science were actually those who were endowed with a special connection to the third field. Einstein, who received many of his ideas through dreams and visions, emphasized that the only way to reveal the fundamental laws and orders of the universe was through the intuition. Anandamurti's fifth layer, the causal body that corresponds to the fourth, cosmic-soul field, is the capacity for a comprehensive perception of the objective world and access to the complete knowledge of the past, present and future. In this layer, qualities, such as eternity, non-attachment, distinction between reality and illusion and spiritual ecstasy, emerge. His sixth layer, the bliss body that is the equivalent of the pure awareness field, is the direct experience of non-causal joy, wholeness, love, and peace, and much more than that, it is a continuous immersion in divine light and oneness with God or the greater reality.

The White Light and the Theory of Subtle Fields

As soon as we comprehend, even intellectually, the Theory of Subtle Fields, the entire logic of the "White Light method" spreads before our eyes, and learning the method becomes an easy and joyful process.

First, we realize that the process of expansion is, in effect, the transition from one subtle field to another, subtler, field. Every element that we expand in our consciousness undergoes a marked process of sublimation, becoming ever more spiritual and liberated precisely because our ability to control the passage between fields—an ability acquired through the White Light—allows it to be steeped in spiritual expanses, which are planes of infinite potential. *Everything is possible* in these planes, and thus, a negative emotion, which suffers from contraction and density, is easily transmuted into a gateway to the divine revelation of the fifth field. Baffling dreams find their solution quickly when they expand into the third plane, in which their unconscious set of symbols can very easily be deciphered. Long-held traumas are absorbed into the third and fourth planes, in which traumas cannot possibly exist, thus causing the person who suffered greatly from the traumas to chuckle while looking down on them from the broader fields. People without any previous knowledge of the fifth field experience states of consciousness that, in the past, were only the shared secrets of monks and renunciates, and people who struggled with a decision they had to make for years are all at once capable of lucidly seeing what they ought to do simply by reaching the third or the fourth fields.

The greatest obstacle in the past was the tremendous effort required to reach these fields, but this barrier no longer exists. The gates to the fields are wide open. We understand that the passage between the fields *is,* in fact, the increasing expansion of consciousness itself.

In the more advanced parts of the book, you will be able to learn how to perform an expansion of a negative emotion by yourself. For the time being, it will suffice to acquire the theoretical basis of such an expansion in order to understand the tight connection between the process of expansion and the passages between fields even more deeply.

In Diagram B at the end of this book, you can see the brain and the five fields as they radiate from the brain and envelope it as five layers of consciousness. Beyond the fields, there lies the infinite reality, and beyond it, the absolute reality abides—which hints at the fact that the fields are really like antennas or receivers through which we get in touch with the invisible reality. Another way to describe it is as five inner senses that are capable of perceiving the hidden dimensions of existence.

The negative emotion begins its journey in the brain and then moves at first expansion into the second, mental-emotional field, which is actually the origin of that emotion. One more expansion may deepen our immersion into the subconscious, which resides in the depths of the mental-emotional field, and thus enable us to unveil the broader emotion, the one of which the surface-emotion was a result, expression, or by-product. A third expansion (sometimes a fourth and fifth are required for this purpose!) will finally lead us to what one may call "the mother-emotion," the fundamental and primordial imprint from which the negative emotion springs.

For instance, if we began with an anger toward our parents concerning some disagreement, the first expansion might lead us to "frustration," the second to "pain," and the third to an "existential need for affirmation." As pointed out earlier, the process of expansion is the process of revealing the fullest potential of each and every element, and as far as a negative emotion is concerned, its utmost potential can be revealed only after the truth in it is totally exposed.

The borders between the fields are highly significant. In many respects, the experience of breaking through a border is like a quantum leap as it is a sudden jump into a totally different plane of existence and being, in which entirely different rules apply and absolutely unique terminology, context, and interpretation of reality are valid. Often, this quantum leap is physically experienced in the most sensual way as if we have jumped all at once over to a mountaintop, to heights and to a climate that we are not accustomed to at all.

The border between the second and the third fields is supremely meaningful. Overcoming it means finally crossing over the psychological domain and shifting into the spiritual dimensions, in which psychology cannot possibly exist. Therefore, their first characteristic is absolute and inherent freedom. Mostly, when a negative emotion is expanded, the expansion following the discovery of the "mother-emotion" will be what we entitle "the neutral state." The neutral state will be experienced as space, stillness, restfulness, and deep relaxation, or, as many tend to phrase it, as "the calm after the storm." This plane is characterized by a silent presence, devoid of drama yet lacking the wonderful and elevating qualities of the third field. In the White Light, we also regard this plane as the structure that, in its expansion, will finally lead us to the transcendental planes beyond time, mundane worries, and the circumstances of life.

As soon as we cross from the mental-emotional field through the neutral state, the negative emotion is transmuted and transforms itself into the sublime positive emotions, non-causal and non-circumstantial by nature, which are characteristic of the mental-spiritual field. Airiness, lightheartedness, unbounded joy, recognition of inherent goodness, freedom, and immortality are only a handful of the qualities that people name in this state as their faces completely soften and begin to radiate the endless light they are meeting from within.

But this does not suffice. We keep on expanding even these structures of emotion and being since the purpose of the White Light is to lead us from a state of contraction (which equals suffering) to a state of absolute limitlessness (which equals bliss). Thus, in the next expansion, many pass through the thin line between the third and the fourth fields, a thin line that is experienced as a "white plane" or as a flooding of White Light. Whether we pass through the White Light or not, at one stage or another, we will reach the eternal states of consciousness of the cosmic-soul field, which exist far beyond all familiar emotions. In the next expansion, the fifth field will finally be revealed, a field which consists entirely of ever-refining layers of the divine state of consciousness, from oneness to infinity, and from infinity to absolute nothingness, and so on. (These are random names; don't get caught in them!).

Only in the fifth field does the negative emotion realize its fullest potential: to lead us to God or to the "source of existence." By completely disintegrating and absorbing into greater expanses, it has ironically drawn us to planes that are far beyond emotion and even far beyond sensation. Of course, in this way, every negative emotion will be considered a faithful servant of the greater reality!

As far as the therapeutic dimension is concerned, the Theory of Subtle Fields may serve as a crucial explanation for the fact that thoughts and emotions, which at the beginning of the process were substantial, possessing a seemingly intense reality, vanish as if they have never existed shortly after starting the process of expansion, so much so that the complainer often cannot even recall the original emotion.

We should keep in mind that the fields embody a much more complex consciousness, but in the same breath, it is also a far simpler consciousness. Through them, we excitedly discover that we can be totally simple and leave behind our familiar plane of thought, which is characterized by disintegration, fragmentation and endless inner contradiction.

The Brain and the Theory of Subtle Fields

The Theory of Subtle Fields is the brain's escape route from its own limitations. Many of us can feel the sidewalls of thought that narrow our possibilities of awareness and experience to a limited number of repetitive and compulsive grooves. Spiritual approaches attempt to lead us "beyond thought" so we may know bliss and liberation, which are our "inherent nature." By having free access to the fields, the brain, at last, can get in touch, systematically and assuredly, with that which lies beyond it.

At this point, we understand that consciousness has a sort of subtle anatomy, of which the physical brain is only the tip of the iceberg: its material extension. It is impossible to reveal the brain's fullest potential without the other layers of consciousness.

Therefore, "consciousness" is a phenomenon that consists of at least three elements: the brain, which is enveloped by the energic-psychic structure (mind), which, in its turn, is enveloped by an even subtler structure that can be referred to as "consciousness" (or "supermind").

In the context of its part within the complex consciousness, the physical brain has a clear role: storing data. The brain organizes information and stores it as memory. The quality of this process in which data and impressions are gathered and categorized is determined by the brain's level of development, and this level of development completely depends on the degree of existence and the activity of consciousness as a whole.

In the absence of consciousness, the brain lacks the ability to receive new and higher impressions beyond the immediate impressions it is accustomed to receiving and interpreting according to its set of memories. In itself, the brain cannot contact the fields of the universe; it will regard them as non-existent and will even mock anyone who claims that there are such fields at all. A brain devoid of consciousness can receive only what it physically perceives and believes it perceives, but as it develops and yearns to tap into that which lies beyond its limits, those complex structures, capable of receiving new impressions, will gradually form around it.

From a certain point of view, one can say that consciousness is a set of skills that the human brain develops with the passage of time. The more it listens, lets go, negates the known and the familiar, and readily opens up to receive new impressions, the more it undergoes a reorganization process, and, correspondingly, a set of connections through which it can contact that which lies beyond it begins to emerge. This set resides within the brain as a dormant potential; without it, the human is nothing more than a physical body and a memory-based brain.

As soon as the brain is properly tuned, the dormant potential of the energic system begins to awaken. The first to awaken is the chakra system, which, until this point, has mainly served as an intermediary between the physical body and the nourishment of the cosmic energy that sustains it. Following the chakra system, the various skills of the subtle fields emerge: a unique and authentic psychic field, an authentic spiritual-self field, the soul and cosmic field and a supreme spiritual field. These fields are capable of conducting cosmic energy, cosmic intelligence, and cosmic awareness into the brain as well as the body cells (through each and every chakra).

The process of expansion can serve as a tremendous catalyst for the awakening of the fields system. It enlivens the chakras and instills cosmic energy into the brain, and thus, like a miracle machine that begins to operate, the brain's dormant potential awakens and initiates contact with the subtle fields. That is why the process of expansion is very often the beginning of man's birth as a spiritual being.

It seems that the pituitary and the pineal glands—which some relate, correspondingly, to the sixth and seventh chakras—play a significant role in regard to the brain's interaction with the fields. Observing the direct experiences of countless meditators, one may posit that these glands carry some dormant potential, which is usually unrealized for the simple reason that it is not essential to man's ordinary functions. The moment the brain interacts with the fields, these two glands are "ignited," and it is very likely that they are the ones that enable contact between the brain and that which lies beyond it, that is, the ability to tap into insight, intuition, foresight, hidden orders, pure cosmic energy, and ever-expanding states of consciousness.

If we liken the fields to nets of light, then, whenever these nets unfold, the two glands become fully operational and function as sensors and receivers of the extra-brain activity. One can assume that at a certain level of man's evolution, these glands would fully awaken and ceaselessly magnetize cosmic activity into the brain.

The Theory of Subtle Fields suggests a far-reaching evolutionary possibility for the human brain: turning from a storehouse of data with a rather poor level of interactions into an abundant and highly active reservoir of intelligence. In the brain's present state, the thought overpowering it is no more than the random activity of memory. Memory accumulates a momentum in the brain until it is no longer merely useful and functional but rather repetitive and compulsive. The memory is the generator of fears and cravings in the human being as it keeps creating associations and past-based networks of symbols. The inevitable outcome is that whenever a man encounters the present, he only meets his past as it is reflected in the present (a point that will be discussed at length in the chapter on the subconscious).

One can go as far as claiming that there is no real present for the human as long as he is entrapped within the limitations of his brain since, within the brain itself, it is impossible to escape from memory's reach or to "leave it behind." This fact puts a serious question mark next to those spiritual approaches that guide the human to be "here and now," without providing a substantial bridge to the "here and now." As far as the brain is concerned, the "here and now" is an idea, a picture, and a symbol, and never a direct experience since the "here and now" lies only beyond the brain in fields that have nothing to do with the activity of memory.

The fields, mainly the fourth and the fifth, are what liberate the human being from the tyranny of memory and grant him a substantial present, a genuine "here and now." In other words, only the fields can free the brain. Considering the fact that the entirety of suffering is a product of the conflict between memory connections in the brain and visible reality, this understanding bears a tremendous significance.

Whenever the brain interacts with the fields beyond time (or outside time), it evolves. Its memory constructs begin to disintegrate; it undergoes a fundamental and profound process of renewal. The fields, primarily the fourth and the fifth, activate the brain in a brand new way: they extricate it from the frantic movement and direct it toward a state of pure awareness. Thus, the new evolution of the brain commences: it is emptied of activity and becomes increasingly illuminated. Its complex of associations falls apart, its pathways of interpretation are persistently removed, and its structures become available as some sort of receivers of higher intelligence.

The "here and now," as well as true wisdom and true love, can be found only outside the brain, within the fields. Otherwise, love will fundamentally remain a biological emotion, wisdom will fundamentally remain the accumulation of knowledge, and spiritual guidance will fundamentally remain mental projections of the brain itself.

The Theory of Subtle Fields, the Universe, and Creation

From a broader perspective, it is possible to upend the flow diagram of the subtle fields and thus to find in it the story of creation or, in other words, the story of divine contraction. Whereas human consciousness *expands* more and more through the fields, the absolute reality *contracts* more and more through the fields until it attains its most contracted state, which is visible (to the naked eye), physical matter.

As a story of creation, the flow diagram will be more or less as follows: before anything else, even before "genesis," there had been absolute reality. This absolute reality contracted itself, at first, into infinite reality and from infinite reality into divine awareness (fifth field). This awareness continued to contract into the creator's intelligence, the intelligence organizing all cosmic orders (fourth field), and this intelligence created the spiritual planes of existence of the third field (the planes of the soul and the basic energic structure of all and everything). The spiritual planes contracted into the mental-emotional plane to enable the structuring of thought and emotion (in the second field). The mental-emotional plane contracted even further into elementary energic and nearly physical structures (in the first field), and these structures contracted into the visible physical form (the inorganic world, biological life, and later on, the human body and brain).

In this way, the Theory of Subtle Fields delineates the great journey of divinity from spirit to matter, and at the same time, offers the human a reverse journey, which is, so it seems, his very purpose of existence: to gradually move from spirit to matter; to increasingly expand from the body toward the infinite being.

These primordial fields of the universe—the divine awareness, the creator's intelligence, the spiritual planes of existence, the cosmic memory, and the universal energy—are omnipresent and all-encompassing. Yet, as a mere body and brain, we lack the ability to get in touch with them. In order to initiate contact with them, we need to develop subtle senses.

These senses are our five fields. Each personal human field can communicate with its corresponding cosmic field. For instance, man's chakras interact with the cosmic electromagnetic field and derive their nourishment from it. Without such a cosmic field, the life force, which is flowing persistently in the body, will abandon the body all at once, and death will be inevitable.

Through the five new senses we develop in the process of expansion. We can communicate with these inconceivable fields, which have existed ever since the process of contraction began yet preceded the creation of man, through several conduits:

- through our physical body, the physical senses, and the brain, we communicate with the cosmic body itself, known to us as the "universe;"

- through our electromagnetic field, we interact with the cosmic field of energy, the pure life force of the universe, and the subtle channels through which this force flows. Our energic body contacts the cosmic energic body;

- through our mental-emotional field, we can communicate with the field of accumulated memory, experience, and experiment of the entire cosmos;

- through our mental-spiritual field, we interact with the field of "astral planes," in which reservoirs of knowledge, insight, wisdom, thought-patterns, and spiritual entities of all kinds reside;

- through our cosmic-soul field, we communicate with the divine brain, the brain of the creator; and

- through our field of pure awareness, we interact with the field of absolute being, the space that holds the space, the pure divine awareness.

The simplest metaphor that comes to mind when attempting to illustrate the reality of the cosmic fields is the Internet. The global human brain interconnects with itself through an internet, without the need for physical bodies. This means that the human has succeeded in creating a mental field that is enabled by bodies and simultaneously does not depend on them. In actuality, what interacts between humans is one's thoughts and emotions with the other's thoughts and emotions, one's computer with another's computer.

Likewise, the interaction between the fields is enabled by the physical body and brain, but, at the same time, does not stem from them. One can imagine the fields as nets of energy, connections of energy that spread out over the entire cosmos. When the brain awakens its spiritual fields, it can finally get in touch with the all-embracing fields of the universe. In other words, it can connect to the cosmic internet, the universal net, and thus initiate contact with that which lies beyond it.

Just like the Internet, the net of fields is non-local, i.e. independent from space or time. This fact bears an enormous significance, as it allows unimaginable interactions with the far ends of the universe and beyond while the human does not move an inch away from his seat. Owing to this, man can connect to the net of cosmic intelligence through his cosmic-soul field and, in doing so, reveal tremendous universal laws. Another example is the genuine "channeler." Such a person possesses the capacity to temporarily connect to the cosmic internet and initiate contact beyond time and space with a specific field of intelligence in the third field.

A man who attains Enlightenment is actually one whose five fields are inseparably merged with the five cosmic fields. In such a state, his brain can interact freely and uninterruptedly with the cosmic fields and, in some respects, conduct the entire cosmos through his consciousness. Before anything else, his awareness is united with the divine awareness and reflects the infinite reality and even the absolute reality.

Throughout the ages, countless people have testified to the power of being in the presence of "enlightened" ones. They have spoken of a magnetizing radiation that has emanated from those extraordinary masters, a radiation which has made them catch the immeasurably profound and ecstatic states of stillness and expansion themselves. Indeed, this radiation is made up of the increasingly unfolding fields of a person who has awakened in his entirety to the dormant potential of the fields.

In the process of expansion of the White Light method, you can experience again and again a temporary connection to the cosmic internet. But one should keep in mind that the enlightened state is a state of uninterrupted connection, in which the human consciousness is united with the enormous universal nets. Then man experiences *himself* as omnipresent and all-encompassing. This state awaits us all as a wondrous evolutionary possibility.

Summary

Expansions are the fastest and most direct way to move through the fields. With every expansion, the brain awakens from within itself the hidden senses of the subtle fields, which, in their turn, begin to interact with the cosmic fields. Then, the brain finds itself fully steeped in a new reality, which in any other condition it would have no access to. In a sense, it is possible to say that the purpose of life is to gather each and every element of our being and to expand it along the fields to the extent that its fullest potential is revealed and can finally materialize.

It is important to note that there is no hierarchy of value in regard to the five fields. Without the fourth field, we will never know the meaning and purpose of life, and without the first field, there will be no energic system to enable the cosmic energy to flow within us in the first place. For this reason, in the White Light method, there are techniques for the development of each one of the fields, and there is no special preference for one over the other. After all, the goal is to attain a state in which we can freely move between the fields, from the most material to the most spiritual and the other way around, never to stop and settle in one field. A person who experiences life from a shamanic point of view, for instance, is one who identifies himself with one layer in the third field, and a person who is passionate only about the space of meditative awareness is one who identifies himself with the fifth field. Nevertheless, the fields are really only one fabric that requires all of the components, different levels and ways of experiencing reality.

The universe, just like our very own being, is a multidimensional existence. When all of our fields unfold, our experience of reality will be multilayered on the one hand and completely free on the other hand. We will be able to identify ourselves with the physical experience as a body and brain in a specific time and space, yet we will also be able to experience ourselves as an entirely spiritual being. Only in this way can the inner logic of life and its meaning be fully revealed.

Now, equipped with the discriminating clarity of the Theory of Subtle Fields, we can explore the five fundamentals of the White Light method.

The Five Fundamentals of Expansion

Fundamental 1: Consciousness Precedes Phenomenon

Through the Theory of Subtle Fields, we learn about a totally new possibility for self-change in every level of our being. We realize that as soon as we awaken the fields, we can settle into them and then act from them. As long as we are "located" in the brain and body, we have a very limited range of action and energy for the sake of self-change. In some respects, we are powerless to act since, being identified with thought and emotion, we try to influence thought and emotion from the realm of thought and emotion; we are like a dog chasing frantically after its own tail.

The Theory of Subtle Fields teaches us that it is possible to awaken new and hidden layers of our being and, out of them, to reshape the "grosser" and more "stubborn" layers (thought, emotion, and physical sensation). When these layers become active, we settle into the part of ourselves that *causes yet remains uncaused, affects yet remains unaffected.*

For instance, the mental-emotional field is a field that shapes the brain's typical pathways of interpretation. For this reason, it is much better to act within its domain in order to alter these pathways than to do battle with the ghosts of the brain itself. Repetitive grooves of thought are now revealed as mere products of fundamental imprints in the second field; they have no independent existence. Thus, instead of fighting these mental grooves, it makes much more sense to simply dismantle the most primordial memory connections that gave rise to them in the first place. However, the best way to affect the mental-emotional field is through the mental-spiritual field since in every condition only a higher and more "liberated" field can actually influence the problems created in the field just below it. Einstein, in one of his most brilliant quotes, maintained, "We cannot solve our problems with the same level of thinking that created them." That is why, in the White Light, we make sure we have settled into the broader field, which contains the more limited field in which blockages were created. (For this reason, the third field is extremely useful for the therapeutic parts of the method as it is located just "above" the second field which is "responsible" for all of our most destructive psychological structures.)

Nowadays, both in science and in the countless methods of alternative healing, it is accepted that the mind can, at least to some extent, influence the body. Positive thinking, meditation, visualization and prayer have all become known means for mental and emotional influence aiming to alter certain physiological realities.

In the spirit of the method of expansion, we expand this idea, too, into the knowledge of the fields, which is far more radical. The familiar principle, according to which "an internal change leads to an external change," turns, in this context, into our ability to act within inconceivable planes, within the subtlest fields available to man and the universe as a whole. Moreover, in the White Light, they become highly tangible and very specific: each plane has a name and a role in the "big picture," and so, we transcend the abstractions that are common in the spiritual world.

Through the process of expansion, we can systematically reach every field. However, expanding alone will not suffice. Expanding means reaching the fields, but the purpose of the White Light is to act from within the fields in highly precise and intentional ways. Each technique in the method targets a different outcome, but whether the goal is untying and dismantling a negative mental pattern, relieving a chronic physical pain, generally transforming the brain's thought structures, or attaining a liberating knowledge regarding the challenges we presently face, the White Light resolutely works from within the fields in order to bring about a visible change on the physical, surface plane.

This is the work of alchemy: acting within the hidden layers of man can, eventually, bring about an immediate or gradual change in the visible layers (thought, emotion, physical sensation, and behavior). In this sense, the White Light is spirit working upon matter. Since the action takes place within the subtle fields, it requires some time before the results come to the surface. Imagine, for instance, an activity that takes place in the fifth field, the field of profound meditation: an activity such as the total renunciation of any want and need for affirmation and love as projected on our close environment. If this activity goes deep enough, then, inevitably, it will affect the rest of the fields. Accordingly, the change will begin to flow from the fifth field to the fourth field, from the fourth field to the third field, from the third to the second, and from the second to the first, i.e. all the way through until eventually the change will reach the brain and the entire body and remold it. Suddenly, the brain will be much stiller, memories will be washed away from it, the perpetual sense of being the "victim" will be reduced, and a new lucidity will allow the brain a greater ability to stand up to life's challenges. In this manner, the fifth field affects our most immediate thought process.

One should understand that the brain and the body, being dense matter, are much slower than the rapidly vibrating spirit. For example, emotion is denser than thought, and physical sensation is even denser than emotion. For this reason, it is easier for us to let go of a belief or an idea we hold dear on the mental plane than to free ourselves from a deep rooted emotion, and for the most part, we find it easier to free ourselves from a deep-rooted emotion than to cure stubborn and incomprehensible chronic pain.

In the same way, the spirit acts upon thought; consequently, thought acts upon emotion; and following it, emotion acts upon the sensation in the body. For this reason, on any journey of self-change, the body "brings up the rear," merely following in the footsteps of the more rapidly-changing planes until, finally, the change catches up.

What follows from this is that the activity within the fields may only yield results on the visible plane after a while. Sometimes, a deep-reaching therapeutic process comes to the surface only after a few weeks. The great advantage of such a process is its holistic action, which removes any possibility of side-effects. The harmony of the broader and more complex fields gradually generates alignments throughout the entire body-mind complex, bringing the complex of the body and mind increasingly closer to the harmony of the fields of the spirit.

In some respects, this is how we can view the system of homeopathy. The increasing dilution of the material leaves only its "memory" or, in other words, only its "subtle fields." These fields are the ones that correspondingly act upon man's hidden fields, particularly the electromagnetic field and the mental-emotional field. After a while, the change in the fields reshapes the physiological and psychological being of the person in a way that is quite safe and free from side-effects.

When a person reaches the fields, settling into them is astoundingly perceptible and clearly distinct from the ordinary settling in the brain and body. There is no need to use your imagination: these layers are characterized by an intense simultaneity (the activity occurs on different planes at the same time) so words can barely contain all that is taking place by a great energy which encompasses the entire being, an energy which ordinarily is not accessible for us through the reservoirs of body and brain; by rapid and effortless thinking, which is unique precisely because of its absence of thought (as we know it); by a direct seeing, free from any need for analysis and the gradual and burdensome dismantling of the "thicket" of our inner world, and above all, by an ability to let go of attachments without resistance or fear. This is not a trance-like state or hypnosis of any kind. It is a bright and clear state of free consciousness, and it is just as we were meant to be from moment to moment in our daily life, too.

It is also possible to relate to the fields in a more physical context—in terms of vibrations or frequencies. The faster the frequency, the less the processes of change require time and processing and the more everything seems possible. Ordinary thoughts and emotions of a slow (linear) nature cannot "survive" in it, and mental activity is far sharper and swifter. Abiding in the faster frequency and acting from within it will make the slower frequency change by adapting itself to whatever occurred in the quicker frequency. In this way, the change eventually diffuses and infiltrates the dense matter of the mental, emotional, and physical planes.

The principle is simple: the quicker the vibration, the more spiritual the state of consciousness. Accordingly, one could think of the creation process as a process of slowing down the vibration until it becomes extremely slow (or, in other words, material). *Matter is a slow vibration of energy*, and, for this reason precisely, its transformations occur much more slowly than the ones we can generate in spirit. Through the process of expansion, we shift to far less dense planes that have extraordinarily rapid vibration, and in this state, we can actually settle into a more primordial plane of existence from *before* the process of contraction and compression that manifests as the thoughts and emotions within us. While completely free on this plane that preceded the creation process, we can create anew, encode the laws of matter anew, and start anew in almost any sense.

Through the process of expansion, we establish the dominion of the consciousness over the material dimension: consciousness precedes phenomenon, and therefore, consciousness can alter phenomenon. It is easy to see how this principle that consciousness precedes phenomenon might serve, in the future, as the grounds for a new medicine and a new psychology. A fields medicine could influence the body from the subtle fields without side-effects and complications, and a fields psychology could remold the thought structures of the brain through the harmonious order of the fields. As the knowledge of the fields is enhanced with the passing of time, many things might all at once become possible.

In my estimation, one of the most significant layers of the Theory of Subtle Fields, as far as therapeutic potential is concerned, is the space of the White Light. This space seems to possess an exceptional power of influence over the planes of mental, emotional, and physical matter, and that is why I dedicate an entire chapter to it.

The validity of the first principle is quite clear to those who engage in transformative spirituality and persistently settle into the subtle fields. Such people know by means of direct experience that the fields truly liberate our brain, heart, and body even if we do not act from them deliberately. This is due to the fact that mere presence in the fields brings about far-reaching transformations in man's visible being.

Fundamental 2: The Fields Are Planes in Which Suffering Cannot Possibly Exist

Suffering—the thicket of memory-based thoughts and emotions—cannot exist beyond the upper limit of the mental-emotional field. Stubborn psychological structures, which seem powerful and even bonded to us in the present developmental plane of our consciousness, lose, all at once, all sense of reality and validity as soon as we shift to a higher plane of development. Each plane is characterized by its own unique range of thoughts, emotions, sensations, terminology, urges, and experience of self, and whenever we leave a certain plane, we immediately separate ourselves from all its contents and find ourselves identified with a totally different range of thoughts, emotions, sensations, terminology, urges, and experience of self.

It would be difficult to exaggerate the significance and implications of this principle. After all, it holds the most substantial key to ending human suffering—not because it resolves the suffering but rather because it invites us to shift to a plane in which the suffering is gone as if it has never been! This implies that if we could only find an easy and fast way to solidly stabilize ourselves in the third, fourth or fifth fields, we would totally bypass the bumpy road of the tremendous effort it takes to unravel our psychological structures.

In the framework of this principle, we clearly distinguish between two paths for coping with the thicket of our thoughts and emotions:

- the "freeway" (the way of the fields); and

- the "dirt track" (the common path to release from suffering).

The highly bumpy, full-of-potholes, "dirt track" is a journey that takes place on the surface of only one plane, the plane of our consciousness as we know it, which is run entirely by our inefficient and conflictual thoughts. On this path, we perceive our psychological state as a state that demands time and an ongoing process of peeling layers. The terminology of this plane includes concepts such as "learning to accept and love ourselves," "appreciating what is," "agreeing to let go," "forgiving," "separating from one's past," "acknowledging the other," and so on. An integral part of the "dirt track" is the fundamental idea of "less" as opposed to "more:" I learn to become a more loving and less stubborn person, who is more attentive and less clinging, more happy and less identified with the victim-mindset. Life is viewed as a set of "lessons" or "tests" in which we stumble upon challenges and learn from them, grow from them, and develop through them our entire being little by little. Often, the gradual dismantling of our inhibiting patterns seems like an unending process. In fact, this is indeed the case as long as we reside in the mental-emotional planes of existence.

While the "dirt track" is characterized by ongoing processes of change, the "freeway" is characterized by repetitive evolutionary shifts from the grosser fields to the subtler fields until a final and complete stabilization within the subtler fields takes place. Naturally, these shifts also take time, processing, and daily cultivation. Yet, in stark contrast to the "dirt track," in the "freeway" one does not deal directly with attempts to remedy and improve the content of thoughts, emotions, patterns, fears and desires of the mental-emotional planes, but rather focuses on the increasing process of expanding the consciousness—out of the clear understanding, based on direct experience, that the more consciousness expands, the more the content of thoughts, emotions and sensations transforms of its own accord, in dramatic, even inconceivable ways. On the "freeway" there is no need to put in an effort to expel the "darkness" only to focus on the light. The very presence of the light expels the darkness.

Personally, I can testify to the fact that, throughout the years of evolution in my own consciousness, patterns of behavior, thought and emotion have vanished (or, to be more precise, have been transmuted) one by one not because I have learned to "forgive" or to "let go" or to "be more trusting" or to "open my heart"—but rather because my consciousness has evolved; my self-identity detached from the brain and the mental-emotional field and began climbing along the broader fields. As a result, my brain has become still to such an extent that any possibility of suffering (which is always created by our own thoughts and emotions) has disappeared as if it had never been.

The second principle teaches us something inconceivable: patterns of thought and emotion can exist only on a certain plane of development; as long as we abide in this plane, these patterns will seem to demand a tremendous amount of attention and slow-going, complex processes of healing, but the moment we escape this plane, they will seem meaningless, even ridiculous.

A person might feel for his entire lifetime like a victim of sexual abuse even if that abuse only took place in his early childhood. For long periods of time, he might wander from this psychologist to that therapist and from this system to that method, and at every stage along the way, he would feel "more and more" relief and "less and less" suffering. He would learn to love himself and to renew his trust in life, perhaps he would even dare to "forgive" the person who attacked him and to find meaning and sense in that traumatic occurrence. This is all very appropriate and becoming on the "dirt track," but on the "freeway," he would find himself in the third, fourth, or fifth fields. There, his entire past would seem quite insubstantial to him, and his experience of self would be revealed as incorruptible and untainted by one memory or another. He would come to realize that, at his core, he is a "clean slate," and that, on this slate, he can create his life anew, without the influence of memory. From the vast spaces, memory itself would now appear as a minuscule dot and no longer as a giant monster consuming his entire being, so the new sense of proportion would alter, all at once, his position in the face of the entanglement that he himself had created through his own fabricated beliefs. He would not understand the point of forgiveness as he would not be able to experience the feeling of the victim, nor would he need any meaning and logic that might console him for his past trauma. He would not need to learn to love himself since his true nature in the fields is selfless love, and he would not need to renew his trust in life since his experience of self in the fields would be one of oneness with life, with no partitions or conditions.

Of course, as already stressed in the first principle, this may require a few more processes within the subtle fields in order to stabilize the new understanding and, most important, to ground it in the emotional and physical planes—spirit and thought are always the quickest to leave the past behind—and still, in the end, this is a significantly shorter process than pointed liberation from one specific trauma, and it has many more far-reaching implications. Indeed, man's being changes as a whole since he gets in touch with a new level of development characterized by bliss, total freedom, fearlessness, absence of want and need, and complete certainty. In other words, the new developmental plane will not merely heal the trauma (or, to be more precise, liberate it from the need for "healing" in the ordinary sense of the word) but will also awaken the dormant potential of the consciousness, the ability to transcend *all* known thoughts and emotions and, in many ways, to become another man.

When a person leaves behind the mental-emotional field and shifts his identification to the mental-spiritual field, he comes to realize that one can grow and develop out of wholeness and happiness and not only out of sense of lack, existential tension, and need. One can mature from a state of happiness toward states of more and more happiness by means of positive evolution.

This refreshing approach toward healing and self-change draws its power from the states of expanded consciousness as revealed by awakened and "enlightened" humans along the ages. Such people did not have to face their psychological structuring but rather developed their experience of self-identity to such a great extent that the entire content of their consciousness totally changed (or transmuted).

In a dialogue between the 20th century philosopher and spiritual teacher Jiddu Krishnamurti and a world-renowned psychiatrist, the psychiatrist at one point confessed that, when his consciousness expands through direct experience, he cannot identify any possible existence of a subconscious on that plane, and hence, there is a state of consciousness in which the very principle of subconscious has no validity whatsoever. The reason for this is that the subtler fields exist beyond the mental-emotional field in which the subconscious resides; as soon as one shifts to the third field, one actually goes beyond the division of conscious and subconscious and moves into wholesome and integrated states of the spirit.

As said in the White Light, we are not content with simply abiding in the expanded states of consciousness but rather we desire to use them in order to reveal the subconscious and to efficiently dismantle it. Supported by the first principle, according to which only a higher or subtler field can radically transform the field below it, we act, from the new freedom, upon the conditioned structures of the brain and the mental-emotional field. Often, a person residing in the expanded fields must be persuaded and convinced to carry out this task of dismantling and purifying the denser fields since his own direct experience (even on the sensual-physiological plane) is that his patterns have completely vanished; he can no longer "remember" that, in reality, he is undergoing a profound romantic crisis or that a horrible stage-fright paralyzed him from head to toe only a short while ago. The thing is that as long as the person has not shifted permanently and firmly into the subtler fields, the moment he comes down from the process he will inevitably return to the contracted consciousness and find, again, his "good old" patterns. That is why it is highly important to use immersion in the fields of eternity to perform the most thorough actions of purification and release.

The far-reaching consequences of the second principle are that its meticulous assimilation will eventually lead us to the post-psychological era, an era in which the psychological paradigm will be replaced with the recognition of man as a consciousness that is capable of the complete transcendence of psychology as we know it. The remarkable insights of psychology, such as the discovery of the subconscious, will continue serving humans but only in enabling a deeply liberating activity in the subtle fields. Further, psychology and spirituality will become one movement in the consciousness, shifting to the expanses of the fields, in which true development does not leave room for familiar suffering.

As previously hinted, one more radical implication concerns the present spiritual paradigm, but we will focus on that in the last part of this book.

Fundamental 3: Expansion Is Bliss

Every component of our being—from our consciousness as a whole to the least of our thoughts, emotions, and sensations—yearns for one and only one state: ever-increasing expansion, a complete shattering of the sense of contraction and limitation, a total liberation from the confining structures of distinct barriers and sidewalls. If one could speak of a positive subconscious, of the suppression of a longing whose nature is mental-spiritual-energic, it could be definitively determined that, in the deepest sense, we, in our entire being, yearn for a state of breaking through limitations and shattering present structures even when these structures provide us, quite successfully, with the security of the familiar and the known.

In other words, unconsciously, we are not content with the stagnation of our consciousness, a stagnation that allows us to properly define our boundaries and our sense of self. In deeper layers of our being, we maintain an ambivalent relation with ourselves, a love-hate relationship, precisely because we are unable to persistently bear the experience of our contracted consciousness. This is our deepest source of suffering. When we become conscious of this subtlest form of suffering, we enter a new journey in our life, a journey of awareness and true development. On such a journey, we progressively discover that true evolution *is* the aspiration to expand more and more, and, moreover, it becomes clear to us beyond all doubt that this expansion, this liberation, *is* the happiness we sought.

The level of happiness, freedom, health, balance and development, increases with the level of the expansion of our consciousness. This is due to the fact that an expanded state of consciousness is also a more harmonious state of consciousness. Harmony in this context means a level that can contain a high degree of complexity without complication, friction, or collision. Whenever the complex of body and mind is absorbed into the more harmonious levels, it is "reminded" of a natural and liberated state, of its own ability to operate harmoniously, and, thus, it slowly but surely returns to healthy and optimal functioning.

For this reason, one's very presence in the spaces of the subtle fields contributes to self-healing and general balancing even before the faintest attempt to act on the body and mind complex from the fields is made. When a person positions himself for two whole hours a week in the expanded states of consciousness of the White Light, he undergoes an unconscious rehabilitation of his entire being, thanks to the fact that the latter gets to learn the natural state of the subtle fields and tune in to them.

The absolute positivity of the fields—a positivity that goes far beyond all pairs of opposites, such as good and bad or positive and negative since opposites can only exist in the grosser fields—encourages the human consciousness as well as the body to let go of any form of negativity. After all, negativity can appear only when there is some sort of contraction. A contraction in consciousness can express itself as an aggressive will which fights reality instead of working with it and growing from it, and a contraction in the body might express itself as an improper flow of blood or fluids, which brings about compression and congestion. The absolute positivity immediately dismantles any negativity, transmutes it, and then assimilates it as a new energy into the fabric of body and mind.

Without deliberate intent, the person becomes in time more peaceful and loving, not from strictly observing moral conduct but rather from the simple fact that anger and hatred turn into states of contraction that the body and mind complex reject. The mind and body complex that has learned a new state of alignment with the laws of the universe from the wholesome and perfect harmony of the subtle fields is no longer willing to comply with the tendency of the contracted thought and emotion toward self-destruction.

The new states "expand" the fabric of body and mind, and, progressively, all of its contracted components "give in" and dissolve into the greater space. As long as the body-mind complex acts in separation and disconnection from any cosmic wholeness, it develops conscious and unconscious patterns of self-destruction. The moment it finds rest and peace within the cosmic wholeness, a wholeness that contains it and nourishes it ceaselessly, it can finally let go of unnecessary struggles and flow freely and naturally without limiting thought and emotion. Just like a lost child who has found his parents, it feels secure and protected again.

Everything aspires to expand and to expose its very core, its potential for happiness, power, and energy. That is why every phenomenon in our consciousness is not only expandable but also worth expanding. Each false thing in its expansion will lead us to the truth, each "dark" thing in its expansion will lead us to the light, and each fearful and desirous state of the self in its expansion will lead us to our truest, most expanded selfhood.

In such a remarkable condition, one in which we know for sure that anything limited may eventually lead us to the unlimited, we will never need to dissolve or repress a negative emotion, a compulsive thought, a fantasy, an addiction, a frustrated desire, or a long-lived trauma. Thanks to the principle of expansion, we are equipped with a powerful tool that can meet everything exactly where it's at in its specific point of development and transmute it into inconceivable states of liberation and happiness in a very short while.

Thus, instead of escaping and avoiding, we learn, in the White Light, to use our most difficult and horrifying patterns to attain infinite bliss. *Whatever kept us in bondage now liberates us.* As we learn to trust the undoubted success of this process—a confidence that can be established within us only as a result of repeated direct experience—we will cease nourishing our subconscious, which is the reservoir of all the elements in our being that we have been avoiding or have been hoping to get rid of, and we will start moving on the healthy route, along which we will unbind only that which already exists in our subconscious until a state of total simplicity is attained.

The first great liberation we will experience in the process of expanding negative emotions and difficult patterns will be realizing the fact that every phenomenon has a limit as every phenomenon is a structure. Yes, *everything* we can ever think of actually appears as a structure within our infinite consciousness—even a tremendous sadness, which we believe would drag us all the way into a bottomless abyss if we only allowed it to.

The truth is that it "feels" infinite only because we identify with it, nourish it ceaselessly, and give it power and energy. Our attention is a powerful element. Turning it toward anything will immediately make that thing substantial and meaningful, and in the same breath, whenever we pull our attention away from something, the latter will lose its power completely. Needless to say, we tend to forget this crucial principle of the power of our attention.

The very fact that we have bestowed attention for many long years on some negative emotion has led to a predicament in which the emotion is experienced as a limitless giant that uninhibitedly controls our being and consciousness. The process of expansion compels us to return to identify the "giant" as nothing but a structure within our consciousness, a structure related to an area in the body, a shape or an image, a color, a general sensation, and a fragrance—and any structure is easily expandable.

For this reason, the first healing that will take place within us will be in our positioning as the consciousness, which can choose whether to give power to something through its attention or to bring back negative emotions or frightful patterns into their proper measures. If the pattern had an independent awareness and existence, you would feel it, at the moment of expansion, sigh with relief, and hear it whisper in your ear, "Thank you. I was waiting for this moment for so long. This is my day of redemption, my day of liberation from my own suffocating limits." It, too, so it seems, is suffering from the exaggerated attention you bestow on it.

There is nothing "bad" that we cannot expand. However, it is not only our attitude toward negative components of our being that must change but also our attitude toward positive components. We tend to be content with circumstantial positive emotions just the way they appear in us, yet the process of expansion teaches us that the expansion of the positive can be a gateway to supreme states of consciousness. Even therapeutically speaking, these supreme states are invaluable. Thus, it is important to understand that not only liberation from the negative can heal us but so can the very process of expanding each and every ingredient within us. An expansion, in many respects, is therapy through light.

Throughout this book you will be able to find examples for various uses in the expanding process. These examples demonstrate the extent to which this process is relevant to each phenomenon and also the extent to which every existing thing may serve our consciousness for the sake of achieving new levels of bliss and transcendence. Emotions or identities, questions or fantasies, memories or symbols, mantras or philosophical ideas—from the point of view of the expanding process, these all await us; await the wondrous capacity of our consciousness to unveil their potential for power, energy, and spiritual fulfillment since the expansion reveals their own most expanded destiny as well, the purpose for which they were made.

Fundament 4: Self-Authority Is the Destination

Constantly abiding by the narrow boundaries of the brain will leave us with a very small chance for genuine individuality. The brain, as long as it does not maintain a continuous interaction with the subtler fields of consciousness, is subject to countless external influences, from which it forms memory connections that dictate the way it interprets reality and choices. Individuality, as we know it so far, is nothing but a misrepresentation of self-authority. As we examine the power of our autonomous being honestly, we realize that it lacks the most important components that define such a level of existence: total freedom of consciousness, absolute self-responsibility, true will, and integrated personality—where "integrated" implies a state in which all parts of the "I" are unified into one holistic "I" that owns a way of thinking and a direction in life that is completely devoid of inner contradictions.

In this way, we all live in a rather strange predicament. On the one hand, we sanctify individualism, and on the other hand, we are capable of fulfilling very little of it—at best, a rather narrow and narcissistic layer, which relies on the psychological revolution as its base. The implication is that if we ever wish to deepen the individual way of life, it will be necessary for us to reexamine the means we possess for its complete and most expanded fulfillment.

In reality, the ability to construct a genuine autonomy can *only* awaken for the first time in the subtle fields. While the brain in its ordinary state of disconnection from the other fields of consciousness is, unavoidably, a structure that is conditioned, influenced, and dependent on environment and circumstances, the subtle fields expose us to a state of being in which we are *completely alone*. Gradually, they allow us to develop the experience of being a source: we ourselves become a source of authority, intelligence, creativity, grace, love, and genuine positive emotions. Such a reversal of experience is not possible within the brain's limits, and from that, it follows that any attempt to develop a true individuality without the support of the fields is, put simply, an illusion.

The 20th century spiritual teacher and philosopher Jiddu Krishnamurti, mentioned earlier, once stated excitedly: "In this there is no teacher, no pupil; there is no leader; there is no guru; there is no Master, no Savior. You yourself are the teacher and the pupil; you are the Master; you are the guru; you are the leader; you are everything!" For many of us, it is easy to think of ourselves as someone who is free from dependence upon a teacher or a Guru, yet it would be a severe mistake to think that this freedom implies true independence—independence is an extraordinary and most remarkable state of consciousness, and, in our days, it is also a very rare condition. Hence, true individuality is a sublime capacity that we should develop within ourselves. It means moving from the state of being influenced to the state of being the influencer, from the generated to the generator, from the created to the creator, from the victim to the chooser, and from the waiter and hoper to the initiator and active participant. Such an evolutionary leap is attainable solely through a solid stabilization in the fields of the spirit.

In order to appreciate the intensity of such a leap, we should understand that its very initial realization is a permanent state of psychological independence from our environment, both positively and negatively: we have no one to blame for our suffering except for our very own thoughts, and we have no one to cling to for our happiness except for our own true self. This is the first necessary step in order to establish our true "aloneness."

Do we totally comprehend and implement the fact that our suffering, from beginning to end, is the fruit of self-creation, that suffering is created solely by our thoughts, emotions, and notions? Have we also assimilated the understanding that no one except for us can liberate us from our thoughts, emotions, and notions? Such an understanding is followed by a tremendous energy, an energy that entirely transmutes expectation, waiting, and the hope for external salvation.

We should keep in mind that hope is the complete opposite of true individuality. Hope can exist only on the plane in which suffering can come into being. In effect, hope is born out of suffering, but as we come to realize that we ourselves create suffering and as we take on the absolute responsibility for disentangling this suffering, hope comes apart and becomes fully transmuted.

While religious people become attached to a hope for salvation explicitly—in the form of a messiah or divine intervention of some sort, and, also, in the form of the world to come and the promise of another life—the secular man translates the remnants of religiosity, which are ingrained in his subconscious, into the hope for some future state of uninterrupted happiness. In his thoughts, he complains about his surroundings and the circumstances of his life and longs to change them progressively until happiness is achieved as a permanent state. Complaint and hope are inseparable Siamese twins, just as suffering and the search for happiness are two complementary halves of precisely the same thought.

From the moment an expansion toward the subtle fields takes place beyond the mental-emotional field, it is inevitable that we will see the naked and simple truth: we alone create suffering by clinging to the confused memory connections of the brain and the second field, and we alone can liberate ourselves by disassociating from the psychological structure and expanding our consciousness further and further. Hence we do not need hope or consolation. Heaven and hell are two states of consciousness created by our choice to identify with either the fields or the brain, and grace is not a divine gift, a reward for prayer or good deeds, but the action of expanding our own consciousness.

We free ourselves through the power of our awareness. Expansion is the only grace there is. Shifting to the fields is a declaration of one's willingness for real maturation, willingness to detach from the collective subconscious, which ties in the seemingly-external suffering and the seemingly-external salvation, and to assume full responsibility for any feeling of tension in life as well as for any feeling of happiness.

In the mental-emotional field, we encounter our unique imprints, our personal subconscious, and our sets of symbols and experiences, but the disentanglement of the mental-emotional thicket depends on our leaping into the third, mental-spiritual field, in which we will experience an unbounded, free selfhood that knows no suffering and is overflowing with non-causal positive emotions for the first time. The third field is a crucial step on the way leading to the construction of "absolute autonomy." We detach not only from frustration, bitterness, and disappointment in regard to the world that allegedly inflicts suffering on us, but far more than that, we finally realize that an inexhaustible spring of all those positive emotions, which we were striving, with great effort, to gather from external experiences, can well up from within us. The moment we experience ourselves as the source of these emotions, we finally let go of the "world" and begin to cultivate ourselves as mature and responsible beings who are not only independent from any external factors but are also capable of reversing the direction of the "arrow" and pouring all non-causal emotions upon external surroundings. When a man overflows from his own core, he finally turns from the state of the influenced into the state of the influencer.

Through the fourth, cosmic-soul field, man develops a selfhood that knows its aim and purpose and that is free to create meaning out of alignment with the cosmic forces and the universal laws. This selfhood is an even more expanded individuality, which is mature to such a great extent that it is connected with what one may call the fields of the infinite creative potential of the universe itself. This means that it possesses the ability to partake in the enterprise of creation and not only make its way as a helpless victim under the enormous and all-sweeping currents of life. In the fourth field, one can speak, for the first time, of "true will." This will directly stems from the principle that determines that the more integrated the parts of the "I" are, the more the ability to make decisions, to choose authentically, and to carry out one's goals increases.

In the fifth field, the absolute autonomy comes into being—a selfhood that embraces the entire cosmos within it and is endowed with an all-inclusive sense of responsibility. Its "I" is the universal, most primordial "I." This is the most earth-shattering level of the autonomous being since man finds himself on this plane in complete aloneness as the divinity itself, which is concealed at the root of his consciousness. The fifth field, the field of pure awareness, reveals to us that God is a state of consciousness, not some force intervening in our lives and guiding us. Of course, what follows from this is that everything depends on us; we are destined to direct life and to "create" it anew out of our own most expanded consciousness.

The total "aloneness" of the field of pure awareness might shake to the core religious people, who have been conditioned to conceive of God in the context of a believing and emotional relationship (within which one may perhaps experience unity with Him but certainly never "be Him"). Nonetheless, if the human species is ever to take an evolutionary leap, it will inevitably be a leap toward assuming complete responsibility, which stems precisely from this unified state of consciousness. Obviously, for this aim we will have to dismantle the memory connections that are the heritage of the great religions within the mental-emotional field, a heritage that has been encouraging us to experience feelings of smallness, helplessness, waiting, and dependency, whereas in our consciousness, a living, grace-bestowing, infinite divinity, like the ever-radiating sun, dwells.

There is no hope outside man. We are the miracle we have been waiting for. The solution for all of our problems is internal: intrahuman, intra-planetary, intra-consciousness. It is fairly natural to be afraid of being alone and of standing on our own feet by ourselves, and yet, we are obliged to take the step and to take up full responsibility for our fate.

To find such solutions on the collective and individual planes alike, our self-authority must develop more and more. Through the expansion of consciousness along the fields and the establishment of our identity in the subtle fields, such an authority can be constructed so that, progressively, a totally independent intelligence may arise from these fields as the result of the interaction between them and the vast fields of the cosmos itself. Nowadays, individuality is like a tiny seed within man; we should expand it in order to realize its power and unique qualities. Even if such a process will demand time and cultivation, and even if the first steps of the birth of independent intelligence will be rather hesitant, the potential achievement in this process is inconceivable: the creation of an immeasurable giant solely through the power of our consciousness.

We start with simple steps; individuality, as opposed to the common conception, is not something one is born with. The ability to "take ourselves in our own hands"—to release ourselves from suffering and to evoke marvelous emotions from within us—is, in itself, a highly significant evolutionary leap. With the passage of time, we are capable, through the expanding process of the White Light, of creating our lives anew: guiding our body and mind toward brand new choices, actions and ways of life.

A White Light instructor will never tell the person who undergoes the process what his own opinion is, what he thinks this person ought to do. Otherwise, he betrays one of the most important principles of the expanding process: supporting the construction of a genuine self-authority, the creation of a true "I," which does not need the instructions of an external authority of any sort. For this reason, the role of a White Light instructor is simply to enable the person to enter into his fields and to position himself in them so that he will be granted the optimal conditions for self-empowerment (gradually, the White Light techniques for *self-work* are meant to habituate the person with the ability of entering the fields and settling into them all by himself).

The expansion has no fixed doctrine or concealed ideas that the person who undergoes the process is expected to "reach." It has no hidden presumptions or prejudices concerning the things the person should do or the ways he should behave and be. The expansion of consciousness has no connection whatsoever to morality of any kind—the "teaching" is being created from within the person, from within his own consciousness in accordance with his present developmental needs, and consequently, it is dynamic and filled with life. Therefore, there is no pretension in the White Light instructor's avoidance of expressing an opinion or position; in the fullest sense, only the person can find out what is truest for him, and his ability to find it out will increase, time after time, the freer he feels within the fields of his consciousness.

Entering into the subtle fields, man will be exposed to the vast potential of his being, a potential that will seem to him completely available and accessible as long as he abides in the fields. However, it is not uncommon for people to find it hard to respond to the prescription of happiness that they give themselves while in the expanded states of consciousness, and this is due to the fact that self-authority is an acquired quality. The more self-authority fructifies and, with it, the more our inner energy and power awakens, the readier we are to take on the full realization of the potential enfolded in the structure of our being.

Fundamental 5: A New Brain Is All We Need

The present brain's focal point of activity is thought. The movement of thought, which is insatiable by nature, is based on memory connections in the brain (as they are partially molded by the mental-emotional field). By "memory connections," we mean associations—connections between one thing and another—which turn into permanent imprints within the memory cells of the brain. It is possible to demonstrate this through a rather simple and superficial memory connection: let's say I am traveling with a friend to a foreign city and the interaction between us on the trip turns out to be disastrous; this relationship will color my entire trip experience, and, as a consequence, crystallize a link between the foreign city and the negative experience—a link that may lead to me refusing to ever go back to that city. Countless memory connections of this sort form within our brain, and then condition and shape it: links between a term and a quote concerning it, between an idea and an experience, between a sensual experience and a trauma, and so on. With time, these connections consolidate, until, eventually, we are barely capable of disconnecting a thing that actually appears in front of our eyes from our memory-response to it. In other words, we encounter each and every thing in the present from our past—from the way the past has conditioned and shaped our brain.

In stark contrast to that, the process of expansion releases the brain from the activity of memory and transports it into a new state: listening instead of thinking. As the brain initiates contact with the fields beyond it, it actually gets in touch with levels of consciousness that are free from memory and, thus, free from conditioning. The freer from conditioning we are, the more the veils that separate us from reality are removed—and a new clarity becomes available for us. Naturally, such clarity can enable the brain to operate uninterruptedly in a holistic, silent, and attentive manner, and therefore, in a far more intelligent and creative manner.

Repeated experience in the fields reveals that true intelligence is not ingrained in the human brain but rather appears from outside of it or beyond it and is only *reflected* in the brain itself. The brain is not demanded to produce anything from within itself; on the contrary, it is required to serve as a reflector or conductor of the intelligent activity that takes place in the subtle fields.

Until an actual connection with the fields is initiated, the brain functions sufficiently, through the mechanism of memory, with its accumulation of knowledge and experience. However, the memory is a limited mechanism, which by its very nature can perceive and comprehend solely what *already was* (and this, too, only partially—in accordance with the conditioned paths of interpretation that filter each experience and draw very little from it). Memory cannot grant an intelligence that is liberated completely from conditioning and limitation—such wisdom lies only outside the brain's boundaries, and it can activate the brain only when it itself disposes of the compulsive habit of using its mechanism of memory as a means of understanding, experiencing and receiving knowledge.

As long as the activity of memory is the focal point, there can be no intelligence. When there is no use of memory, when the brain completely abandons this mechanism, extraordinary intelligence, wakefulness, clarity and lucidity will emerge all at once. Indeed, one could say that memory is the protective layer that divides and disconnects the brain and the subtle fields. There are spiritual teachers who assert that "freedom of consciousness lies in only a one-thought-distance"—and, truly, this means that freedom is just one memory away from us. Beyond memory, wondrous, vibrating fields of energy stretch without horizon; beyond memory, the greater, wholesome life, which can be contacted only through the subtle fields, exists. As a human brain, we should contact this life, which is unattainable within the reach of memory. When the activity of memory ceases to function as the center of comprehension and perception for the brain, the borderline between the brain and the fields of consciousness is breached, and thus it can finally get to know the real life.

The expansion neutralizes this memory mechanism and pulls the brain out of it. All structures in consciousness are, in effect, memory connections; therefore, the moment a structure is expanded beyond its limits, it "leads" us beyond memory and conditioning. This is precisely why a person who suffers from a certain trauma—an exceptionally entangled and complex memory connection that inhibits the blossoming of entire realms of life—reaches a state in the subtle fields in which he has no connection whatsoever with that trauma. Actually, he can no longer "remember" what exactly provoked his excitement and shock so greatly in regard to a rather negligible past event. The inability to recall what was there before is tremendously significant.

The very existence of pain or stress within the fabric of body and mind is the outcome of the memory mechanism. Without memory, a subconscious is completely insubstantial, and stubborn patterns of thought, emotion, and behavior lose their validity. For this reason, the fastest, most radical therapy is releasing the brain from the activity of memory, an act which indirectly results in liberation from suffering and patterns. Through the fields, we come to realize that there is no actual need to toil over the disentanglement of patterns but rather only to shift the brain to this new state of pure, memory-free listening. The shift to a new state of brain's activity is life-changing in any dimension one could think of.

The process of expansion aligns the brain with the fields which exist prior to memory and which lie beyond memory, totally independent from its activity. In this way, it gradually erases, as it were, memory from the brain and the cells of the entire body—and this erasure of memory allows the brain to conduct, in ever-increasing power, the tremendous intelligence of the subtle fields.

Liberation from memory allows the brain much more than the transmutation of its suffering-producing mechanism. A brain in a state of pure listening can see reality without distortion and interruption by unconscious motives, and therefore, it can also directly face "what is" as it is, without hope, escape, condemnation, or justification. This fact makes the listening brain, compared with the thinking brain, immeasurably more efficient and creative when it comes to solving problems and breaking through barriers of all sorts. When we closely examine this, it will become clear to us that obstacles that appear in our life are nothing but a reflection of obstacles within our consciousness, which stem precisely from unresolved memory connections. In such a predicament, it is wiser to remove the blockages of consciousness—to unravel the memory connections—and, as a result, to clear enough space for an incredible clarity that can cope with any objective situation at the speed of light.

Stillness, the absence of any motion in the brain, is a far more intelligent state than thought, which is turbulent, conflicted, and filled with inner contradictions. The moment the brain observes some situation without reaction and immediate interpretation, it allows itself to remain holistic and integrated, and in this way, it can capture the situation in its entirety. Then, the brain will realize that, without any effort, the answer or the solution lies within the very heart of the situation and surely not in its own entangled and confused storage of memory.

The very effort to think on something so as to attempt to solve it entraps the brain in its own limitations and compels it to turn to the memory drawers in desperation, hoping to extract anything of value. But how creative can the brain be as long as it tries to solve a situation through a quite irrational fabric of fears, confusion, desires, unconscious motives, and memories from similar experiences? If we keep in mind that thought is memory, and, therefore, thought, by its very nature, is conditioning, we will deeply fathom the importance of the unconditioned brain in regard to accurate and wise decision-making.

No person can truly decide whether to stay with his partner or to leave him or her as long as his brain is molded by the fear of loneliness, by the desire to control the outcomes of each and every action or by environmental pressures of all sorts. The brain must be empty in order to encounter the pure solution, which rises from the depths of the situation itself.

The memory connections are not solely psychological. A whole range of memory connections exist, both individual and collective, that completely condition and limit our communication with the supreme truth and with the answers to life's greatest questions. These connections stand as a veil between us and the objective, real knowledge that lies beyond the boundaries of the brain and even beyond the boundaries of our personal fields of consciousness. When the conditioned brain encounters the term "truth" and is convinced that it "knows" what it is—based on some heritage and on the certainty of accumulated knowledge—it actually turns the "truth" into an idea that is entrapped within its limits and misses the chance to initiate contact with the real life that exists behind this concept.

The process of expansion also releases the consciousness from the reservoir of memory connections that revolve around knowledge, and in doing so, shifts the listening brain to a state of unification with fields that have nothing to do with belief and tradition. In these fields, the brain finds itself completely alone—an authentic state that enables it to get in direct and independent touch with that which, too often, the heritage of knowledge and fixed philosophy only keeps away from.

The brain, being alone, independent and unaffected, and free from memory and conditioning, can create a new reality, a reality that stems from a genuine present. It is easy to see how the emergence of such a brain might assist us not only in a new creation in our individual life but also in the broader aspect, that of the evolution of mankind: as long as the brain is conditioned to what is already placed in its memory storehouses, it will approach the challenges of the present—such as hunger, discrimination, and poverty—from the conclusions of the past, while a new brain might get in touch with new solutions for old problems and offer uncharted paths, along which we can tread toward a genuine and unconditioned future. For this reason, in many respects, the quality of consciousness is the factor that might determine our future not only as individuals but also as a race that inhabits this planet.

The process of expansion itself never conditions the brain to "this idea" or "that conclusion." On the contrary, its entire aim is to provide an opportunity for free exploration, which, the more the consciousness itself expands, might also develop time after time. The journey of expansion is a journey that does not have, and cannot have, an ending since our consciousness is infinite by nature.

It seems quite plausible to daringly argue that constant, ever-increasing contact with the unconditioned fields makes the brain itself evolve. Without a shadow of doubt, it becomes flexible and, also, more complex. Perhaps, old connections come apart in it, and new connections take their place. Also, perhaps, a dormant potential (among others, the dormant potential of the pituitary and pineal glands) awakens and begins to operate—or even gets to be created *ex nihilo*. One way or another, the direct experience is intelligible:

when the brain gets in touch with that which is beyond its limits and begins to operate as a receiver of higher truth, new energic capacities, which connect it to the fields that surround it, appear. This implies that the process of expansion might be found, with time, to be responsible for a significant part of the development of human consciousness.

5

What is the White Light Energy?

Although the realm of the White Light, which is revealed in the borderline between the third field and the fourth field, is only one layer of many found along the fields of consciousness, I have chosen it as the symbol of the entire method. In this chapter, I will explain why.

At the beginning of this book, we learned that the external senses have completely parallel inner senses, which allow us, among other things, to characterize different structures and identify their shapes, colors and fragrances. In precisely the same manner, the physical light—known to us as the light of the sun, fire, and artificial lighting devices—has a completely parallel inner light. Naturally, this light is invisible to the physical eye and can be perceived only through intra-sensual experience. Nevertheless, a significant resemblance exists between the sun's light, which radiates over the entire planet, and this hidden spiritual light: just as the light of the sun enables and provides life—and, correspondingly, symbolizes life in our consciousness—so, too, the spiritual light is a substantial, as well as symbolic, source of life.

Throughout the ages, all over the world, practitioners of meditation have shared the experience of a dazzling White Light that has flooded their being from within and that has seemed to be "brighter than a thousand suns" (at least, according to one of the common metaphors). This White Light has turned, in the meditative realm, into one of the typical symbols of our "true self," a sign that we are approaching direct and profound contact with the divinity within us. Nowadays, we may use a more accurate set of concepts and explain this through the expansion of consciousness along the fields that surround the brain; nonetheless, the direct experience has remained, to this day, one and the same.

In near-death experiences, persistent reports tell us, many experience the sense of walking or floating (or even being magnetized) toward a gleaming White Light, being absorbed into White Light, and encountering light-radiating beings. This light is interpreted, within the bodiless consciousness of the temporarily deceased, as forgiveness and unconditional love, and, also, as the erasure of the past and the promise of a new life.

When it comes to our collective subconscious, paintings from every tradition and era visualize angels or supreme masters—from Moses to Jesus—as either being encompassed by White Light or radiating it. In the New Age culture, everyone speaks of "light" and "love" in the same breath; even when those people lack direct experience with the light, they still intuitively sense its realness and nature.

Many healers know the secret of the White Light and use it in order to bestow a purifying life energy on their patients. Thanks to the expansion process, we can now activate, fully, the fourth principle—the principle of self-authority—not only to freely experience this plane within us and as us but also to put this energy, which has become totally available to us, to use. From now on, it will be rather easy to unite with the plane of the White Light and to be supported by it as a regenerating, transmuting and releasing light, which can work its wondrous action on nearly every level of our existence.

As already mentioned, the White Light plane is the borderline, the barrier that separates the spiritual dimensions of the third field from the divine orders and dimensions of creation of the fourth field. This light, which glows directly from our high self—which may be regarded as the "soul"—and directly from the spiritual heart of the cosmos, is a purifying and healing force that deletes memory and past and promises a new life. When a person encounters it and becomes absorbed in it with his entire being, he is granted the life-preserving nourishment of the inner light, just like a person who comes out of his home into the world and is flooded with the warm and rejuvenating light of the sun.

This direct experience of nourishment, healing, and erasure of the past is truly the experience of an extremely high and subtle level of love. Hence, it is also possible to regard the White Light as the energy of spiritual love. Each time we contact it, it sends the message of a new beginning, a possibility of a new life. When contacting this spiritual energy, it dissolves every difficulty and resistance within us—in the body, emotion, brain and heart—and, essentially, makes us feel purified, unblemished and good.

The greatest gift of the White Light is that, by being absorbed into it, a sense of knowing, which says we are *already good,* appears. That is, our process of development does not have to be a process of "self-repair," but rather growth out of a sense of wholeness. Through the White Light, we come to learn that, on a more expanded level of consciousness, we are completely and impeccably whole, and this can be our starting point for every further step we might take in our development.

On a very deep level of our collective subconscious, a fundamental existential tension lies. Among the sources of this tension, we can include a few memory connections: the existential tension of the predator-prey relation, the fight for life and the struggle for survival, the tension of the original-sin consciousness and the fall from heaven, and the tension of countless societal prohibitions and taboos of all sorts. The direct implication of this tension in the psychological experience of each and every one of us is a very primal feeling of being "not-good-enough," a feeling that conveys to us that we must strive very hard in order to fix ourselves in order to become good and worthy. This is quite inevitable; after all, the great myth that molds the minds of so many of us—the myth of Adam and Eve—is the telling of the beginning of humanity as a sin!

In stark contrast to the common belief, this existential tension is anti-evolutionary and does not foster any kind of healthy growth and maturation. On the contrary, it dramatically withholds the human and makes him freeze in a state of self-condemnation and self-hatred. Fortunately, as soon as a person encounters the plane of the White Light, he all at once experiences forgiveness and a deletion of the past without correcting his wrongdoings or promising to be "better." The White Light tells him that his very being is good and complete and that the myth of heaven and hell is false since true spirituality deals with evolution and not with sin and morality and hence, nothing has ever been accumulated against him—in this very moment, he can experience himself as a clean slate, write his life anew and raise his gaze toward an horizon in which actual opportunities and chances are spread out. For this reason, we use the instruction to wash our entire being with the White Light in the method again and again, including thought, emotion and sensation, and particularly, the parts of the body that are entrapped in some agonizing memory connection.

The more the person abides on the plane of the White Light, the more he is literally steeped in the light and the more he heals his miseries on every level, particularly his guilty and unworthy heart. He feels purified and renewed, owing to the fact that, on this plane, he is accepted, loved, and real in essence—a spiritual being in essence. Above all, he learns that he does not need to make an effort to be and that development is not gained through effort as we know it, but rather through the cultivation of silence, which is the total cessation of all efforts.

The White Light releases the person from the sense of effort that society implanted in him. It allows the "abolition of debt" and enables the person to feel unblemished, and innocent, to dare to feel that he did nothing wrong, even when he acted immorally, and to agree to feel the inherent justification and affirmation of life.

As said of all things, it is the assimilation of the principle of evolution from wholeness—instead of evolution from lack, tension and need—that allows the person to enter a genuine path of development. Until then, whatever seemed to him to be evolution was nothing but persistent attempts to overcome the great suffering ingrained in self-anger and condemnation, the suffering of his inability to accept the goodness inherent in his very being:

"I'm complete. I'm good. I'm pure. I'm innocent. I'm real. I exist. I am allowed. All is well. There is no problem. I can start anew. There are no barriers and limits. I'm new. The past is erased." This is the fundamental knowledge that is revealed to us on the White Light plane, and from the moment of its emergence, it starts generating a transmutation in the centers of body, emotion, brain and heart. It has only one goal: to transmute the basic existential tension into a fully positive feeling, a feeling of wholeness and completeness that is ingrained at the core of one's being and does not need to be gained or acquired.

To make development along the fields possible and to enable the brain to leave behind the memory-based planes of suffering, one must start anew, as if nothing has ever happened. The plane of the White Light grants us this sense of beginning. Thus, being the ground of any genuine evolution, the White Light has turned into the symbol of this entire method. In this light, we can see how the White Light plane demonstrates three out of the five fundamentals of the method:

- Whenever we activate the healing and rejuvenating potential of the White Light, we put the first principle into use—"consciousness precedes phenomenon." The purification of our depths generates transformations in four centers: body, emotion, brain, and heart.

- The profound logic of growth out of a sense of wholeness and positivity draws its power from the second principle, according to which, "the fields are planes in which suffering cannot possibly exist." We do not need suffering, pain and existential tension in order to want to evolve. It is the other way around: we can allow ourselves to evolve from the positive toward the more and more positive.

- The fourth principle, "self-authority is the destination," is realized here, radically, as it is revealed that the grace of the White Light resides in the depths of our consciousness and does not lie outside us at all—neither in the hands of some powerful healer nor through some hidden divine touch. In the most radical sense, we are able to heal ourselves.

Almost every technique of the White Light can lead to the plane of the White Light. Almost any expanding process can lead to this wondrous plane that resides between the third and the fourth fields. The names given to it can be different and still be rather similar—names such as "the white space" or "an expanse of complete illumination." At any rate, the direct experience will be one and the same: all-encompassing spiritual love.

You may have noticed the slight intimation: the White Light is, in effect, the emotion of love in its expanded state. For this reason, the easiest way to reach this plane is by expanding the emotion of love; whenever we experience this emotion, we are actually connected, to some extent, to the White Light.

As humans, we were destined to experience all possible levels of love—from the most biological and "material" love, to love as a pure state of being. As we view the experience of love in accordance with the Theory of Subtle Fields, we can discover its complete range:

1. On the physical plane, we experience biological love. This love lies beyond our ability to choose and is controlled by the tremendous force of biological attachment. We experience it primarily in relation to our parents and children. There is an arbitrary dimension in it: in the hospital, they might have accidentally replaced our baby with another, and still, we would feel toward the child the same incredibly intense sense of responsibility, caring, and total involvement in his life. When a person to whom we were attached in this form of biological love dies on us, the body itself mourns for the loss, as if part of it has been cut off and will never again regain its sense of wholeness.

2. In the second, mental-emotional field, we experience emotional love and intimacy that is not based on the force of biology, such as a romantic relationship, friendship or creative collaboration. These relationships have a dimension of choice and intentionality in them, and they compel us to grow up, in order to willingly sacrifice our shortcomings and drawbacks. We learn to overcome our selfishness, which is deeply rooted in the memory connections of our subconscious, and to expand toward the other, *out of choice.*

3. In the third, mental-spiritual field, we may find ourselves in a relationship with what can be regarded as a "twin soul;" a far more spiritual connection that crosses over the boundaries of time and space, and in which, we are genuinely interested in supporting the true development of the other and not in preserving his superficial personality. Moreover, thanks to the awakening of non-causal emotions in this field, we will experience a state of selfless and overflowing love that is not based on neediness toward others but rather on our wish to benefit them and to give ourselves over to them.

4. In the lower limit of the cosmic-soul field, we will find the plane of the White Light—love as nature and not as an emotion toward others. Here we begin to experience love as an essential and no longer as an emotion that depends on others or on circumstances. This love does not awaken as a result of something in the external world, but rather is derived from no less than the most foundational motive of our existence. We are motivated by love, and it is also our meaning of life; our purpose is to realize this love in any way that befits the unique soul structure as it is revealed in the fourth field.

5. In the fifth, pure awareness field, love is a direct radiation of our true being. We are moving away from the experience of love as an emotion altogether and discovering

ourselves as a totally autonomous sun, which shines its light, out of perfect selflessness, over all that is. Any action arising from that sun is actually an effortless radiation toward those that happen to be in its surroundings; it "loves" without "loving," simply because it is there, overflowing.

As already stressed, the development of consciousness along its fields is the "freeway." On the "dirt track," we attempt to remedy the selfishness in our relationships, whereas, on the "freeway," we expand our consciousness to such an extent that all levels of denser love are being balanced and aligned with the highest level, that of the fifth field. As a result, the more contracted layers get into their right proportions and are also released from unnecessary psychology. The implication is that there is no need to overly toil over the small details of the relationships—the fact that they are distorted stems from our selfish and needy level of consciousness; our conflictual consciousness is what puts them into conflict.

A young man who came to the White Light with the intention to treat his difficulty with fitting in socially, was disappointed to find out that, of all things, his instructor insisted on inquiring into his very need to be loved and to receive the recognition of others. Expanding this need, he discovered that the right action was to be found in the very opposite: it is he who can abound in love toward everyone else. Hence, the issue is not social blending, but rather a reversal of self-conception, which at once provides him with the ability to become, himself, the one who gives.

On the "freeway," moral laws, such as "love thy enemy" or "love the other as you love yourself," are being fulfilled of their own accord, not because we make an effort to comply with them, but for the simple reason that this is how the expanded consciousness behaves; this is its most spontaneous action. From this, it follows that, on the "freeway," such manifestations of love are but indications of the level of consciousness and are no longer sublime moral principles. After all, on the "freeway," concepts cannot exist—there is only the actuality of the living being, moment by moment.

6

Enlightened Psychology: A New Definition of Mental Health

The theory of the subtle fields and the five principles of expansion lay a foundation for a completely different psychological approach than the one that has molded and conditioned our brains for the last hundred years since the Freudian revolution. When psychology—the comprehension of the psyche, which enables the healing of its ailments—takes into account the whole gamut of the five layers of consciousness, it discovers not only a far more complex structure of the human psyche but also new and excellent ways to untie psychological knots and achieve genuine emotional and mental recovery.

For a start, it is a matter of proportions: as long as we perceive the psyche as if it is all there is, it will appear infinite in its layers and complexity; our subconscious might be pictured in our mind as a bottomless abyss. Owing to the broader view of the subtle fields, however, we can go deeply into the different layers of the psyche and use the different aspects of these fields to unravel each and every knot within them. As soon as the prime content of the psyche—conscious as well as subconscious—constitutes, in addition to the brain's memory reservoirs, one and only one field (the mental-emotional field, of course), it finds itself in a relationship with the electromagnetic field "below" it, as well as with the three subtle fields "above" it. In this way, the enormous and disproportionate magnitude of the mental and emotional patterns, as we experience them too often, is replaced with a rather pale and scanty presence; the mountain turns into a mouse—and this alone is already an initial yet significant step of recovery. Before anything else, in light of the fields and the principles of expansion, the very term "mental health" completely changes—in the language of the White Light, it *expands*—and accordingly, the final destination of the therapeutic process also changes and expands.

When Freud was asked the purpose of psychoanalysis, he responded that it has two purposes: the first one is to enable the person to work and love, and the second is to lead the person to a state of "ordinary human unhappiness"—the more common state of human misery. In the White Light, mental health will be considered the optimal and harmonious activity of *all* components of consciousness, and on no account, the removal of a disturbing "neurotic" element and the return of an unbalanced individual to function in the world. The meaning of this is that, when a person enters a process in the framework of this method, the instructor's goal is not only to help him dispose of the neurotic factor—a compulsive thought, a deep-seated and abysmal fear or an incessant and disproportionate emotional need—but rather to awaken, in the entire fabric of the body and mind, repeated feelings of health, alignment, integration and harmony, until it "learns" them by itself and embraces them as natural states.

When the system reverberates with the wholeness and freedom available in the subtle fields of consciousness, it becomes clear that there may be a state of "mental health" which far exceeds its wildest hopes and imaginations; a state in which the body is no longer overly alert with existential tension and persistent, unconscious, survival signals, and in which the life force (first field) flows freely and uninhibitedly; the brain is still and empty of circular and purposeless thoughts (second field); non-causal positive emotions burst from the depths of being itself (third field); at the core of being, an understanding of meaning and direction of individual life, as well as life in general, is immanent (fourth field), and awareness itself is totally free from the various worldly phenomena and rests within the infinitude of the cosmos (fifth field). In other words, the very definition of "mental health" expands along the fields, until, eventually, we realize that the body, the brain and the five fields of consciousness must operate optimally and harmoniously for us to be truly healthy; "safe and sound" in the full sense of the term. The implication is that as we educate ourselves to shift to a new plane of all-out harmony, we can create conditions in which all types of psychological ailments simply cannot possibly exist anymore.

New Layers of Therapy

The tangibility of the fields also shatters the conditioning according to which healing must be "psychoanalytical"—that is, the result of delving into the recesses of the mind and deciphering them. Now, we understand that it is not only that mental and emotional complications can be solved through absolutely non-psychological means but also that often there are totally different dimensions of our being that require "healing." Therefore, psychoanalysis might turn out to be no more than a misdirection and a distraction from the real challenge.

Many meditation practitioners can testify to the fact that certain patterns of both the mind and body—such as compulsive thoughts or addictions—have vanished as if they had never been as a result of their practices. This means that patterns often come into being as by-products of boredom and emptiness, a lifestyle that does not provide an answer to deep needs of the psyche or an impersonal existential tension that is devoid of any "psychoanalytical" content. Undoubtedly, a whole range of mental distortions exist in man that are not meant to find an answer in the form of psychological decoding—whether by an expert or the self—and perhaps they also cannot be answered this way.

The "Logotherapy" method of the known psychologist, Viktor Frankl, is a fine example of a psychological approach that rejects the psychoanalytical principle as the answer to all needs of the psyche. According to this method, the most profound "subconscious" of man is, of all things, a positive subconscious. Its base, its primal driving force, is the desire for meaning (in stark contrast to Freud's "pleasure principle" and in an interesting parallel to the *desire for expansion* of the White Light): the unconscious drive of man is to find a substantial meaning to his life, and in this meaning, he might also find great relief for many neuroses. This is due to the fact that "the spirit of man is not mere mechanical machinery" and that man is, first and foremost, an entity whose "prime aspiration is to realize meaning and fulfill values and not only to satisfy urges and impulses."

In his important book, *Man's Search for Meaning: An Introduction to Logotherapy*, Frankl determines that, very often, the neurotic man "attempts to evade the full recognition of his life mission. Insisting on his mission, opening his senses to a fuller recognition of this mission, might greatly contribute to his ability to overcome the neurosis." He altogether rejects the psychoanalytical suspicion in regard to man's search for "himself" and for his "meaning," and claims that such existential frustration is not a mental illness, but rather a spiritual distress. For this reason, existential despair is often not truly solved by taking narcotics or even by exposing the unconscious psychological origin of the despair (trauma at the age of three, for instance). The effort to turn off this despair and to bring about a tension-free state totally misses the despair's concealed message. The very opposite is true: this existential frustration, which may be a generating factor in the formation of various neuroses, can be resolved only by facing the completely justifiable spiritual problem. In this manner, the proper treatment will not be psychotherapy but rather a therapy that "dares to penetrate into the spiritual dimension of human existence." In this kind of therapy, the disentanglement of existential frustration will not take place, necessarily, by means of self-understanding—it might take the form of direct actions, the greatest of all would be accepting the burden of responsibility for finding and fully realizing a meaning to life.

Of particular interest, is the case that Frankl presents to support his claim—the story of an eminent American diplomat who came to his office in order to pursue a psychoanalytical treatment he had started five years before with a different psychoanalyst. Frankl asked him why, in his opinion, he thought he was in need of analysis, and the patient responded that he was not satisfied with his progress in work as he found it very hard to endorse American foreign policy. His former psychoanalyst had claimed that the US government and his superiors had represented father figures for him and that his resentment toward his position was caused by his unconscious hatred for his father; thus, the solution would be to attempt reconciliation with his father. Now, after five years of analysis, the diplomat's mind was completely tangled with too many symbols and visions. In the session with Frankl, he finally reached the rather simple insight that his aspiration for meaning was thwarted by his occupation and that he actually desired to engage in a different job. After shifting to the new job, the neurotic problem was completely solved. From that, Frankl derives: "Not every conflict is necessarily neurotic" and, therefore, "the true role (of the doctor), is to help navigate the patient through the existential crises of his growth and development." His important conclusion is that, in many cases, "it is not the wallowing of the patient in himself... that breaks through the vicious circle; the key to healing lies in his commitment toward himself!"

This example of the Logotherapy method shows that the solution for psychological suffering does not always lie in unbinding subconscious symbols or in raising repressions to the surface. In effect, the range of solutions for psychological suffering expands the more our conception of man's essence and human potential for transformation expands. Hence, perceiving man as the owner of a vast consciousness, which stretches over a brain and five subtle fields, opens many new channels for us, through which we can tackle the psyche. Existential frustration due to a continuous disconnection from a sense of meaning might be resolved in the fourth, cosmic-soul field, and not only that, it would be impossible to answer it by rummaging through the subconscious of the mental-emotional field, even the complete silence of the fifth field would only repress it more! At the same time, we cannot necessarily solve a fundamental existential tension through more doing in the world, and it is very likely that, in such a case, the field of pure awareness would be the *only* solution for the dissolution of the tension. Such a profound attitude toward the many components of the whole human being allows for all-inclusive listening to the different and versatile needs of the psyche. (One particular guide for self-diagnosing these needs will be given in the chapter, "The Chakra System and the White Light," though it is important to keep in mind that, in most cases, this will demand the experience and wisdom of a certified instructor of the method.)

As pointed out at the beginning of this book, contraction implies suffering and expansion implies happiness. Correspondingly, the psychological approach we are familiar with narrows down the person and his chances for happiness, whereas an approach that identifies depths in man, far deeper than the memories that are buried at the bottom of the subconscious, grants him, prior to the beginning of the therapeutic process, an opportunity for healing through the positive and not through the negative. This must not be taken lightly since optimal results are not the only important thing in therapy—no less important is the psychological-spiritual-philosophical standpoint of therapy in regard to life as a whole, as it will inevitably mold the minds of those treated in its framework.

Absolute Positivity As the Ground for the Therapeutic Process

As already explained in great detail in the second principle of the expansion process, the White Light's therapeutic action never takes place in the mental-emotional field, but only *from* subtler fields *toward* the mental-emotional field. The inevitable implication is that the sense of absolute positivity encompasses the entire process: brimming with unconditional compassion, love and joy, we approach our subconscious, our most painful emotions, our most delicate traumas, and from this state, we disentangle the thicket. Only absolute simplicity can resolve horrible complication; only a state free from psychology can heal psychological connections, and only a lucid brain can let go of a compulsive thought. For this reason, the White Light process is usually not accompanied by bitter tears or any other kind of cathartic outlet—the all-containing silence emerges within us as a new level of maturity, which can easily dismantle the structures created by the former, more childish level. After all, catharsis is the complementary opposite of an ongoing stressful state in the body and mind, and in silence, the body and mind cannot be tense at all.

Psychology's attempt to exchange one thought for another (or, alternatively, a thought for an action) may only quench our thirst for liberation to a certain extent. The moment we encounter the ability to replace thought with *a liberated state of being* in which thought, as well as its opposite, cannot possibly exist, we realize, for the first time, that the ultimate purpose of any genuine psychology is liberation from psychology altogether. The idea is not to forever wallow in the psychological layers of our self, but rather, to already feel free, and out of this freedom, to escort these layers toward their final redemption—which, of course, awaits them in the subtle fields.

This is the meaning of the term *Enlightened Psychology*: the entire therapeutic course of action is not founded, at all, on "problem consciousness." A woman undergoing a White Light process compared her experience of this method with her experiences in psychological treatment:

"When I had attended psychological family-therapy with my child, and, for a prolonged period of time, individual treatment, they spoke so much about the "problem," that it became the only thing that existed: we became the "problem"—I was narrowed down into being nothing but a "problem," and that was how I started perceiving things, and also, that was all I started communicating to my child. I became a frustrated and blaming person, frustrated because "treatment does not solve the problem" and blaming because it seemed like the others were the ones who were creating the problem. As a consequence of the treatment, communication turned into blaming and attacking, and qualities that used to pervade our home—acceptance, love and compassion—simply didn't receive any attention. The White Light amazed me since I discovered a state in which, instead of me being wholly the problem, I myself was joy, lightness, happiness, silence and flow—even when the challenge still existed simultaneously! I have simply expanded—and when you're expanded, the whole notion of a problem falls apart." Another woman writes: "I had attended psychological treatments for long periods of time between the ages of seventeen and thirty five. I ended up more complicated than I had been when I entered these treatments: a great residual stress accumulated in my mind from referring to myself as an unsolvable problem; like a leader of a country that is totally conflicted against itself, in which the maximum relief that is possible is "cold peace," living in peaceful compliance but with ongoing, moderate suffering. During the psychological treatment, I didn't discover even a thread I could follow to untie this great entanglement, only a capacity to analyze it, which, surprisingly, gave me nothing but more complications. In the White Light, I was finally released from the belief that a therapeutic process must be experienced so negatively."

The Power of the Expanded Self

One more important principle of Enlightened Psychology, which follows from everything we have discussed until now, is that, in this psychological approach, a great deal of focus is given to developing an integrated and vast self, which by its mere presence can immediately solve many patterns of the psyche.

Even though in everyone's display window a witty, fluent, and decisive self is proudly presented, in actuality, our true selfhood does not yet exist. An unambiguous indication of that is to be found in intersections of decision-making where we encounter many voices within us that are conflicted with each other. These voices are, in effect, different layers of the "I" that operate independently and disconnectedly within the fabric of body and mind. The result is that we are more like a whole orchestra without a conductor than a single instrument that virtuously plays its own tune.

When we speak of true selfhood, we must not confuse the bunch of ideas, thoughts, and emotions with which we identify with a total presence of being that does not at all require any "existential confirmation" by ideas, thoughts and emotions of any kind. Interestingly enough, the very absence of such a presence brings about the creation of many psychological imprints. Since the body and mind are empty of a strong and integrating presence, they easily fall prey to the crystallization of negative impressions. In like manner, the mere emergence of such a presence is enough to make the body-mind complex discharge any kind of distortion and imbalance.

We can get in touch with a hint of this through the following little exercise: since we are not present, a stream of thoughts and memories is incessantly attacking us and flooding our mind, so try, with your entire being, to wait for the next thought in order to catch it and examine it with your fullest attention. Very soon you will come to realize that whenever you await the appearance of thought, it cannot arise, and only at the moment in which you let go and forget about the whole thing will the stream come back to your mind. In other words, thoughts and emotions can exist only in a state of absence of attention and lack of wakefulness, and they cannot exist when your awareness is fully present.

According to this logic, the increasing emergence of the integrated, expanded and genuine self (of course, out of the third, fourth and fifth fields) is therapeutic in itself, and often there is no need for more than that. Such a self can be liberated independent of techniques or any form of external salvation, and in its presence not only are ancient negative impressions thrown away from the system but, also, new negative impressions can no longer form. From this point of view, it is possible to relate to the entire subconscious as the assemblage of impressions that come into being in the absence of true self.

In this context, too, we can point to the power of change that new proportions grant us: the true self "overcomes" the content of the mental-emotional field, simply because it is vaster and the entire content of the field is held within it as a relatively minuscule point in an infinite space. Negative impressions, which are pictured in our mind as enormous in measure and depth and which demand years of meticulous psychoanalytical disentanglement, are met, on our part, with a chuckle the moment we properly expand our selfhood and observe them from it. Then we recognize the simple truth that our attention is a far greater force than any emotion, thought or memory, and that all those negative impressions appear to be powerful only because we have nourished them with a great deal of energy and attention—and this means that, in the absence of that energy, that constant fuel, thoughts seem like thoughts and emotions like emotions; they are quite powerless and neutral by nature. All we had to do was turn our brain's attention toward the subtle fields beyond all thoughts and emotions. Thus, a self that constitutes a counter-answer to the hyper-sensitivity of our contemporary soul, which is shaken by any slight gust of wind, be it internal or external, gradually consolidates in us.

Further, Viktor Frankl points out:

> A given symptom evokes a phobia, the phobia activates the symptom and the symptom increases the phobia. A similar chain of events we find in compulsive and obsessive cases, in which the patient struggles against ideas that incessantly visit him. But in his struggle he reinforces their power to bother him since pressure draws counter-pressure, thus again the symptom is strengthened. On the other hand, when the patient ceases to struggle with his obsession... the vicious cycle is cut off, the symptom grows smaller and eventually dies away. In the fortunate case, in which there is no existential emptiness calling to be filled by a symptom, not only can the patient successfully mock his neurotic fear, but he will eventually be capable of ignoring it altogether.

The subtle fields, being total freedom from the mental-emotional field, exist beyond the self-nourishing struggle and also beyond the "existential emptiness calling to be filled by a symptom." For this reason, they are the supreme healer of the psyche.

Supporting a Genuine Emotional Development

Another major problem resolved by the fields is our substantive difficulty to tackle such greatly irrational emotions while the center of gravity for our being is placed in analytical, rational thought. We tend to encounter this obstacle during a psychoanalytical process, be it one that we go through under the supervision of a psychologist or one that we do to ourselves out of habit and conditioning.

At this stage of human evolution, emotions exist within us as a repressed layer of being. Above it, the layer of thought subsists, increasingly thickening owing to the growing use of rational, intellectual and logical tools. The result of repressing the emotional layer is constant dissonance: we know how we should behave and think, and we "understand" a lot, but for some reason the stubborn and rebellious emotions go on behaving in their own way and do not accept the authority of our intellectual understanding. With great embarrassment we look at our angers, fears and irrational reactions, and we do not know how to deal with them in a way that will allow them a substantial release. They are just like tiny babies screaming unendingly, and we, who try to help them, have no way to tell what it is exactly that they are asking for in their odd language. Eventually, we do our best to suppress them as much as possible, while desperately trying to understand what happens to us in all those moments in which they erupt uncontrollably. As a direct result of this oppression, the emotions become twisted and turn into neurotic thoughts that threaten the display window of rational thought more and more.

In the present reality, there is no way for emotions to undergo a development of their own. Emotions cannot evolve through intellectual comprehension; there must be direct access to them, access that allows them to go through a transformation from the plane on which they actually exist. For this reason, even when we "understand" why we behave one way or another ("This is because of the trauma I experienced when I was two years old" or "I react in this way because I inherited this pattern from my father"), we still cannot act differently, or, alternatively, we do act differently—while our body and emotions storm within us and pound relentlessly, drawing us toward the totally opposite direction. Thanks to the power of our rationality we are ready to step up to the stage and speak up, even when we suffer from stage fright, but we do it while our heart beats furiously and all our body signals tell us that we are in nothing less than a life-threatening situation. In other words, the body and emotion remain as they are and we compel them, by the power of cold logic, to engage in actions that are completely unnatural for them.

It is in the power of the Enlightened Psychology, which relies on the fields and the expansion process, to work with the emotions where they are and to allow them, at last, to evolve. The most important thing is cultivating our ability to directly contact the emotion, bypass the analytical thinking and agree to contain it without justification, condemnation or repression, and this, of course, can be done only when we know for certain that we will not "drown" in it since we are equipped with proper tools for transmutation. The expansion works on the material that the emotion is made of and dissolves and transmutes it into the subtle fields so that it gradually turns into a positive energy that totally supports and accelerates our developmental journey. In this way, emotions are not waste that we need to dispose of but rather a wonderful raw material for transformation; there is no need to "heal" them but rather to allow their evolution. Owing to the fact that not only is there no need at all to avoid difficult patterns but, to the contrary, they can be used to attain infinite happiness (as we learned in the third principle, "expansion is bliss"), we can tread lightly and fearlessly on the path of emotion that leads us, step by step, toward our final illumination.

Psychological Work without the Sense of Difficulty and Effort

Among mankind, there is quite an inevitable apprehension (also originating from the psychological conditionings of our times) that an enlightened psychology, founded on fields and expansion, might turn out to be a new form of repression. Such expression of concern is perfectly understandable since, compared with the experience of difficulty and the obstinate "stonecutting" of our rock-like personality known to us in ordinary psychological work, expansion is characterized by a sort of unbearable ease.

For a moment, we will ignore the fact that, in the White Light, too, a highly meticulous and thorough activity is available for us in regard to every pattern of our being—after all, the difference between the method and ordinary psychology is only in the nature of its activity and its location within man's being—and we will examine this worry in itself.

Our greatest conditioning concerning psychological work is the belief that the process of unraveling a difficulty must be shrouded in an atmosphere of difficulty; if we feel lighthearted, happy and joyful throughout the process—perhaps even lighter and happier than we have ever felt in our life—we believe we might miss the seriousness and depth of the whole thing. A feeling of joy, bursting out of the depths of our subtle fields, makes us identify, in an instant, long-lived conflicts as ridiculous thoughts—all that seems superficial, like some sort of self-deception, or something "too good to be true" in our mind. We are afraid not only to flatten but also to realize that we have fooled ourselves; we are afraid that the moment the "magic powder" of the expansion process disappears and we return to our ordinary state of consciousness, we will experience the pain even more intensely now that we know there is another reality.

First, it is important to understand that the fear of repression is but another form of repression: repressing the positivity and the freedom that is completely accessible to us within the depths of our being. Secondly, we should reexamine the psychological habit of incessantly rummaging in each and every pattern—it may be that this habit only deepens and reinforces narcissism and self-focus, which eventually only worsens the neurotic state. There exists a substantial possibility to expand a pattern, make it disappear in a way that is independent from time and process, and, within a few minutes, go on with one's life lightheartedly, free from the burden of psychology. We ought to remind ourselves that entire parts of the psychological state of being are self-creations that are constantly reinforced the more we turn our gaze "inwardly" in worry. Not only that our problems are not progressively resolved the more we delve into them but rather, they become more complicated and entangled because of that and even bring about new neuroses.

In the end, this common belief—the fear of repression that arises upon encountering the Enlightened Psychology—is yet another cornerstone of the "dirt track." This track is the way of suffering, the way that leads to "ordinary human unhappiness," and it presumes that liberation from suffering must also involve some kind of painful process. It is hard for us to imagine that positivity will change us, whereas, in reality, there might even be a path in which we do not deal with "boldly" and "penetratingly" tackling patterns at all but only move along a spiritual route enhancing our inner light, a light that, in itself, dispels all darkness; such a route shifts from positivity to more and more positivity, and it is as valid as any other path.

Any route, whatever its nature may be, demands cultivation, seriousness and depth—and, in Enlightened Psychology, commitment to the process is also an essential element. Therefore, it would be quite childish to be disappointed at the inevitable moment when one leaves the fields at the end of the expansion process and returns to ordinary level of consciousness. It is obvious that this return should occur, and for the time being, until we manage to settle into the subtle fields with the whole of our being, we can use the tremendous power of immersion in the fields, even if it is limited in time. Even if we are not free to move along the fields whenever we feel like it, still, the action that we have performed on a pattern from the subtle fields might prove to be highly effective and lead to a "remembrance," within the fabric of mind and body, that the "freeway" is indeed the right approach to coping with life and with the complexity of our psyche.

One of the most compelling experiences I have ever had in regard to Enlightened Psychology was at an event guided by the developer of "The Work" technique, Byron Katie. In a live demonstration, she summoned to the stage a young Israeli man who, in childhood, had undergone a murder attempt by a group of terrorists. These long moments, during which he had experienced the horror of death in the face of the murderous intent of the terrorists—until he was miraculously saved by passers-by—accompanied him throughout his entire adult life as horrifying, living memories. Byron Katie chose to handle his case from an extremely surprising angle. As is well known, one of the four principal questions of "The Work" is "Is it true?" and Katie was using it now, facing the memory-ridden guy: "I was almost murdered by terrorists"—"Is it true?" This was her question! In an instant, I was struck by the insight that she was attempting to draw his consciousness toward an expansion, toward fields in which this memory was inactive and therefore completely invalid. This was a remarkably bold step since she aspired to awaken him to a dimension in which he was totally free from the memory itself (and therefore, of course, needed no therapy at all). The terror-stricken man resisted Katie's suggestion to put his memories to such a test—if he had done so, he would have encountered the stunning possibility of an existence, here and now, devoid of any molding and conditioning trauma.

This is an excellent example of the actual possibility of an inconceivable release that might appear as the repression of a highly significant trauma. What is more, one can argue that, even if at that very moment he would have responded that the memory was not true, the trauma would have re-attacked him later on. But if this were indeed the case and the trauma would have re-attacked, it would have been, then, an invitation to go back into the fields, surely not to become so frightened as to return to the agonizing dirt track. The fall from freedom is a call to deepen one's commitment to the freedom that was discovered, and it would be a grave mistake to interpret this as a proof of the meaninglessness of such states of being. Now, thanks to the expansion process, we are equipped with the ability to go back to the expanded states by ourselves, and we no longer have a reason to become disappointed and sink back onto the safe and comforting "dirt track."

In sum, these are the fundamentals of Enlightened Psychology:
1. The psychological structure is nothing but a small part of human consciousness—a fact that, on the collective level, changes our present psychological paradigm, and on the individual level, grants us new and healing proportions in regard to our psychological problems.

2. Mental health is an optimal and harmonious activity of all components of consciousness.

3. In accordance with 2 above, it may be that the healing we require is not related to the mental-emotional field but to completely different fields, and additionally, it may be that psychological problems in the mental-emotional field can be solved only in other fields (for instance, a spiritual problem can be disguised as a psychological problem).

4. Throughout the therapy of Enlightened Psychology we experience ourselves in a state of joy and happiness. Of all things, this position of our being can assist us in handling the "problem" in a new way (without a sense of problem!). A therapeutic process does not have to be strenuous and painful: we are allowed to feel, before anything else, free and happy in the subtle fields, even when a problem exists simultaneously, and thus experience ourselves free at the beginning, middle and end of the process.

5. The ultimate purpose of psychology is a release from psychology. We escort the psychological layers toward their dismantling in the subtle fields out of the understanding that, in essence, we are not psychological creatures at all.

6. The complete presence of true selfhood is a therapeutic step in itself, which possesses the power to dissolve many patterns *as a by-product.* The subconscious is, in effect, the assemblage of impressions that come into being in the absence of true self.

7. Enlightened Psychology treats the presence of the hardest patterns "positively" and is ready to meet them without condemnation or the mediation of diagnosing thought. In doing so, it is capable of extricating them from a long-lived repression and assisting them in developing and transforming.

7

The White Light for Emotion — Expand It Yourself!

At this stage, after we have comprehensively studied the process of expansion and after we have assimilated the most fundamental principles of Enlightened Psychology, we are prepared to experience the "White Light for Emotion" by ourselves. This technique is in fact the do-it-yourself derivative of a far more complex technique, which is for the use of a certified White Light instructor. The purpose of the do-it-yourself technique is to enable you to guide yourself through quick therapeutic processes whenever in need. They do not purport to be able to perfectly disentangle highly complicated patterns but rather grant you the possibility of elevating yourself moment to moment beyond your emotional and psychosomatic blockages toward planes of true psychological health.

In the independent study version of the "White Light for Emotion," we experience the expansion of a negative emotion for the first time. It is possible that during the expanding process for a positive emotion at the beginning of the book we came across the difficulty of allowing ourselves the privilege of feeling happy beyond imagination, and yet, the expansion of a negative emotion is more challeng-ing. This is for a few important reasons:

1. *We are not used to disconnecting and isolating the emo-tion from the situation that "evoked" it.* Our misconcep-tion tells us again and again that it is the situation in the external reality that causes emotion: my husband made me angry; the drivers on the road caused me constant stress; the people who gossiped about me made me feel insulted. However, in actuality, our set of emotions al-ready exist prior to an occurrence, and the latter only brings them to life in the form of automatic reaction (this will be discussed at-length in the next chapter, which is dedicated to the way our memory connections are the sole creators of our psychological suffering). The first step of a genuinely liberating therapy is always tak-ing on full responsibility for our suffering: a profound understanding that we create suffering through our in-terpretation of reality, an interpretation which is totally distorted by our emotions and beliefs. Of course, this does not mean that suffering exists only within our con-sciousness—after all, the consciousness of humans cre-ates the world as we know it, a world in which everyone inflicts suffering on everyone else due to the distortions of their consciousness. Hence, the world is indeed un-justifiably hard, violent and cruel, and yet, this does not mean that we cannot be completely released from our suffering-inducing psychological structures and live in a totally positive state in such a world. This is just how powerful our consciousness is! If so, we have to get used to the act of disconnecting and isolating emotion from occurrence in order to understand that there is no need to analyze the occurrence and examine how to deal with it—in effect, any attempt to "deal with" the occurrence, as long as we have not dismantled our emotions toward it, is a grave mistake. As far as we are concerned, *any moment in which we feel tension means that we are expe-*

riencing a distorted reality—no tension can ever be justi-fied! We ought to remind ourselves of this whenever we are tempted to bluntly place the blame on someone else and to develop irrational expectations. As soon as our consciousness is whole and spotlessly perfect, we will know how to tackle the situation without much difficulty. It is all about balance and silence. From all of that follows that the very act of disconnection from the external occurrence is, in itself, a great release and a great responsibility—a sober act of examining our distorted perception before any action or reaction in reality.

2. *We find it hard to agree to be with an unpleasant emotion and contain it.* The simple law is that we cannot be truly liberated from anything that we are afraid of, intimidated by and or trying to escape from. If we wish to be released, we must agree to meet the thing itself face to face and, moreover, to envelop it with our quiet awareness. The built-in survival tendency of an organism, whatever it may be, is to pursue pleasure and evade pain, but here we transcend this tendency and agree to contain the "unpleasant," to feel it from the inside and to know it in its depths. Only profound acquaintance with the negative emotion will allow us to properly reveal its structure, and as mentioned, it is only possible to perform an expansion through exposing the structure. So take a deep breath and sink into the emotion without getting caught in any one of the extremes: intensely identifying with it or, alternatively, condemning it and attempting to repress or remove it. We tend to believe that if we resist emotional pain and "hold on tight," it can shield us from pain, but of all things, relaxation that contains the emotion builds up a genuine invulnerability in us. In the process of expansion we even go as far as to take one more step, encouraging the emotion to grow stronger and spread all over the place, and in this way, not only do we reveal its structure in a greater clarity

but we also increase our ability to endure and contain, and consequently, increase the presence of our more expanded selfhood.

3. *We find it hard to let go of the emotion, as unpleasant as it may be.* Every psychological phenomenon within us has its complementary half, and this section is the complementary half of section 2. As befits our fragmented thought, which is laden with inner contradictions, we always waver between two extremes: identification and condemnation, an overly intense expression of the emotion and an attempt to repress it, and clinging to it yet yearning to be released from it. Due to this devious duality, we too often find it hard to be freed from something that causes suffering. This has more than one reason—one significant reason is the fact that deep inside we know that we will lose something the moment we are liberated from the emotion, for instance, our sense of being the victim, which we recognize as our last remaining sense of power. Another important reason is the fact that, after all, an emotion is also a thrill, and therefore, even when it comes to a totally unpleasant emotion, it still seems far more dramatic and exciting than the state of a liberated, mature, responsible and complaint-free being! Hence, it is highly important to reveal these motives, which may certainly hinder the process of expansion, within ourselves.

4. *We find it hard to conceive that certain emotions may indeed have a limit.* At least a few emotions within ourselves seem to be no less than infinite, like a bottomless, wide-open abyss, and if we sank into it, we would find ourselves entrapped in an eternal hell of pain, fear or sorrow. But if we dare to try, we might realize that our very willingness to enter the "thicket of darkness" with our entire being enables us to discover that an emotion has an edge and a limit; even the most intense emotion "asks" to exhaust itself. The great philosopher

Jiddu Krishnamurti had mourned his beloved brother who died at a young age from severe illness for three days and three nights—he had incessantly cried and screamed out of the agonies of separation, but thanks to his totality, the three days of mourning ended up in a rebirth; he actually "expanded" the sorrow to its maximal limit, and beyond it, discovered the eternity in which death has no reality at all. It is important to remind ourselves of this fact and to insist on finding out what is beyond the limit. Even if at the beginning of expansion the emotion seems endless, take it into account that every structure has an end. When we bestow great attention and energy of identification on an emotion for many long decades in our life, it accumulates its own momentum and turns into a sort of independent entity that deceivingly seems even bigger than the measures of our consciousness and our body, but, fortunately, exposing its structure reminds us that the emotion is smaller than us after all and exists as a structure within our consciousness.

5. *The pain hurts us, and we want to skip it and rush to the positive plane in which it feels much more "pleasant."* It is possible to deceive in the process of expansion, but we only deceive ourselves. If we try—due to a deep-seated pattern of avoidance of pain and emotional intensity— to lightly skip the emotion and leap, through one quick expansion, to a positive plane, we are making a great mistake since any genuine process demands honesty and sticking to the stage in which we really are. It is better to go through seven negative expansions and to rightfully earn the positive plane after that than to quickly identify the emotional structure so that we will not overly feel it. On the other hand, you will be able to notice how, from one expansion to another, the number of circles or layers does diminish—the reason for this is that your ability to leap from one field to another becomes enhanced.

This is a good sign for the development of consciousness, provided that it occurs organically, out of profound honesty and sticking to the process just the way it is.

6. *Along the expansion process we are "thrown" back, again and again, to negative emotions—we do not seem to succeed in persistently advancing through the positive stages of the expansion.* There are three possible reasons for "zigzagging" along the expansions. One is that in the early stages of the expansion process our mind is distracted and we find it hard to maintain concentration for a prolonged period of time. A much deeper reason is the body-mind's "resistance" to the positive planes. This "resistance" is, before anything else, neural and physiological: it is difficult for us to conduct such a positive and vast state for a long time, so we must repeat the process again and again until such a capacity is developed. The third reason is the fact that the light of the expanded fields brings about a process of purification and an elimination of psychological toxins from the body-mind fabric, and therefore we might experience a dual state in which the core of our being abides in a totally "enlightened" state but negative emotions, images and memories flicker somewhere in our peripheries. In such a situation we ought to remind ourselves that these negative elements are being purified from the system, and therefore they should not distract our attention from the center of happening in the consciousness. We are so used and conditioned to ascribing tremendous importance to passing emotions and thoughts that often a rather humorous state appears in the White Light process: while man's consciousness is fully steeped in an infinite space beyond description, his attention is still attracted to the ghost of a tiny ephemeral thought.

7. *We find it hard to imagine that we can really go back to "reality" and act in it without the familiar emotion.* We tend to identify with the structure of the automatic

reaction of the emotion to such an extent that we no longer possess even the slightest trust that we can ever experience our *selves* separate from it. For this reason, the technique is not content with experiencing the free state, but also insists on providing observations from the subtle fields of the various layers of the emotion and on delineating a new attitude toward them. This action generates not only a disassociation from the emotion but also a penetrating and liberating vision into its very heart from a far more intelligent state. The technique is also concluded by a detailed description of the way we might act now, from the free state, so as to ensure that even if the experience of expansion fades away, there remains a "heart-knowing" in regard to the more authentic course of action for us. The advantage of the "heart-knowing" is that it can survive all circumstances, states and times, and it is independent from our transient experience. That is why whenever we disconnect from the fields at the end of a structured White Light process, there is the instruction: "You can choose to keep in contact with this state within your heart even in your ordinary state of consciousness." Again, the big problem is our cynicism in regard to our ability to *live* whatever it is that was revealed to us—and this cynicism should, in itself, undergo a specific process of expansion until it dissolves completely (from experience, it is very likely that you will trace the roots of cynicism to a deep-seated pain that lies at the bottom of your subconscious).

8. *Shortly after the process of expansion, which grants us relief, the occurrence returns to overwhelm us with the emotion.* This is very likely to happen not because the expansion process is ineffective but rather because we have given the emotion a tremendous amount of attention and power of awareness for many long decades, whereas we have only given the subtle fields one or two chances! We should understand that in order to reverse

the huge momentum of the emotion we need to dedicate the same level of attention and power of awareness to the subtle fields through the process of expansion. Now the fields should turn into a daily habit, until they manage to overpower any emotion, pattern and limiting memory. And yet, we must keep in mind that the power of the "White Light for self-work" is not similar to the power of precise therapeutic work with a certified White Light instructor; there are patterns ingrained deeply in our psyche, in the form of memory connections, that are heavily entangled and far from the reach of our superficial awareness, and so it is recommended to untie such patterns by more skillful means.

The following do-it-yourself version of the "White Light for Emotion" is suitable for your immediate application. The moment some tension appears in your life, triggered by some external or internal occurrence of any kind, you can close your eyes and carry out the expansion process until you reach the subtle fields, where you can abide to your heart's content.

At the beginning of the process, you will be guided to isolate the negative emotion from the "story" or "drama" that encompasses it and to shift it, through expansion, from the brain and body to the second, mental-emotional field. As you go more deeply into the expansion process, you will be able to penetrate the layers of the subconscious from which this emotion stems. Along with the expansion, you will finally arrive at the "neutral state," which is, in effect, the borderline separating the mental-emotional field from the mental-spiritual field. The neutral state is characterized by a sense of peace, silence, space and deep relaxation—the "quiet after the storm," as it were. One more expansion after this may already send you up to the mental-spiritual field, toward non-causal positive emotions, and from there, as you go on expanding, you can go far more deeply into the subtle fields, to brighter, freer and more expanded states of being.

Thus, we may start the process with our anger at a comment our mother made, which we interpreted as an insult:

- At the first expansion, the anger may transform into frustration (second field).

- At the second expansion, the frustration may transform into the need for confirmation (second field).

- At the third expansion the need for confirmation may transform into the longing for warmth and communion (second field).

- At the fourth expansion the longing may transform into relaxation and quietude (neutral state).

- At the fifth expansion the relaxation may transform into wholeness and completeness (third field).

- And from there onward, one can move on from "wholeness" to White Light (between the third field and the fourth field), from White Light to "Liberated Being" (fourth field), from "Liberated Being" to "Infinity Consciousness," and so on.

After we settle into a broader state, we encounter the emotion in a deeper, more thorough way. We do not content ourselves with the expansion process but rather perform a short activity within the mental-spiritual field as well—observing the different layers of the negative emotion from the expanded state of consciousness, and afterward, performing an integration of the observations through the delineation of a new course of action in reality itself.

———————————

Practice: The Expansion of Negative Emotions

Whenever there is a need to transmute a certain emotion, close your eyes and follow these instructions.

1. Breathe slowly and deeply. Allow your body to relax more and more with every breath you take... Open up to this process, in which you are about to discover that this emotion has far deeper roots than the present

situation in which it appears... Feel yourself more and more as a peaceful and vast awareness, which allows any emotion, sensation or thought to really be, blossom and fully express itself—an awareness that can peacefully contain everything with no resistance whatsoever, simply because it is wide enough... Most likely, you are accustomed to either identifying with or condemning this feeling; however, this time allow yourself to feel the emotion fully and deeply with no judgment or reaction; allow it to be so you can truly get to know it... Breathe into the emotion, feel it deeply, and move toward its depth...

2. Now allow a certain moment in which this emotion is strongly felt to appear in your mind. Let this moment arise by itself, with no control or deliberate choice making on your part. Feel the emotion as it appears within the scene. Where are you? ... Describe what you feel, think and experience during this event... Choose a general name for your feelings in this event—the most dominant and accurate emotion... Examine where this (... general name) appears the most in your body...

3. Breathe into the (... general name) as it appears in the scene. Agree to feel it fully, even if there is some resistance in the body and mind to fully contain it... Now disconnect the (... general name) from the scene and remain only with this feeling, using the area in the body in which it was felt the most. Be with it. Sit in its very center... Then, bring up the scene that aroused the feeling again. Feel the (... general name) as it appears in it... And, again, disconnect the (... general name) and remain only with the feeling. Breathe into it... For the last time, bring up the scene that aroused the feeling. Feel the (... general name) as it appears in it... And, again, disconnect the (... general name) and remain only with the feeling. Breathe into it...

4. Feel deeply the (... general name). Move toward its center, into its very core. Try to describe it in words. What does it feel like? ... Look for an area in the body that is deeply connected with it... a shape or an image... a color... a sensation... a fragrance...

5. Now feel the (... general name) from within. Breathe into it and allow it to spread wider and deeper. Let it fill your entire body and being. Breathe into the (... shape or image) in the (... area in the body), and let it expand more and more, until it reaches its maximum limit, until it cannot expand anymore. Request: "(... general name), show yourself completely to me!" ...

6. Give a name to the expanded emotion... Feel the (... expanded name) deeply. Move toward its center, into its very core. Try to describe it in words. What does it feel like? ... Look for an area in the body that is deeply connected with it... a shape or an image... a color... a sensation... a fragrance...

7. Now feel the (... expanded name) from within. Breathe into it. Allow it to spread wider and deeper. Let it fill your entire body and being. Breathe into the (... shape or image) in the (... area of the body), and let it expand more and more, until it reaches its maximum limit, until it cannot expand anymore. Request: "(... expanded name), show yourself completely to me!" ...

8. Give a name to the expanded emotion... Feel the (... expanded name) deeply. Move toward its center, into its very core. Try to describe it in words. What does it feel like? ... Look for an area in the body that is deeply connected with it... a shape or an image... a color... a sensation... a fragrance...

9. Now feel the (... expanded name) from within. Breathe into it. Allow it to spread wider and deeper. Let it fill

your entire body and being. Breathe into the (... shape or image) in the (... area of the body), and let it expand more and more, until it reaches its maximum limit, until it cannot expand anymore. Request: "(... expanded name), show yourself completely to me!" ...

10. *Keep on expanding (sections 8-9) until you reach a state in which there is no impression of the negative emotion; a state which is characterized by peace, space or freedom. This is the neutral state.*

11. From this state, return in your memory to a time and a place in which the (... last negative emotion, just before the neutral state) did not exist within you—you can often find such a time during your childhood or infancy, but it is possible that you will have to go back to the womb or even to the time before conception. Where are you? ... What did you feel at that time? ... Give a general name to this feeling... Where in your body do you feel this (... general feeling) the most? ...

12. Breathe into the (... general name) as it appears in the scene. Agree to feel it fully, even if there is some resistance in the body and mind to fully contain it... Now disconnect the (... general name) from the scene and remain only with this feeling, using the area in the body in which it was felt the most. Be with it. Sit in its very center... Then, bring up the scene that aroused the feeling again. Feel the (... general name) as it appears in it... And, again, disconnect the (... general name) and remain only with the feeling. Breathe into it... For the last time, bring up the scene that aroused the feeling. Feel the (... general name) as it appears in it... And, again, disconnect the (... general name) and remain only with the feeling. Breathe into it...

13. Feel the (... general name) deeply. Move toward its center, into its very core. Try to describe it in words. What does it feel like? ... Look for an area in the body that is

deeply connected with it... a shape or an image... a color... a sensation... a fragrance...

14. Now feel the (... general name) from within. Breathe into it and allow it to spread wider and deeper. Let it fill your entire body and being. Breathe into the (... shape or image) in the (... area in the body), and let it expand more and more, until it reaches its maximum limit, until it cannot expand anymore. Request: "(... general name), show yourself completely to me!" ...

15. Give a name to the expanded emotion... Feel the (... expanded name) deeply. Move toward its center, into its very core. Try to describe it in words. What does it feel like? ... Look for an area in the body that is deeply connected with it... a shape or an image... a color... a sensation... a fragrance...

16. Now feel the (... expanded name) from within. Breathe into it. Allow it to spread wider and deeper. Let it fill your entire body and being. Breathe into the (... shape or image) in the (... area of the body), and let it expand more and more, until it reaches its maximum limit, until it cannot expand anymore. Request: "(... expanded name), show yourself completely to me!" ...

17. *You can keep on expanding (sections 15-16) as much as you would like. When you feel fully immersed in the expanded consciousness, move to section 18.*

18. From this expanded state, wash your body, emotion, thought and entire being with light... Ask your body-mind complex to align with this state: "transform yourself into the light of this expanded state!"

19. Now, feel that this state is also a vast container in which everything arises and subsides. In this container you can clear and enlighten any pain or confusion that keeps you away from this expanded state.

20. From this state, look deeply into the (... last negative emotion, just before the neutral state). Examine what the source of the pain and difficulty of this layer of emotion is... Examine what it is that you really seek in the event that aroused this emotion... Keep on looking until the deep reality of the emotion becomes completely clear...

21. From this state, look deeply into the (... medium negative emotion). Examine what the source of the pain and difficulty of this layer of emotion is... Examine what it is that you really seek in the event that aroused this emotion... Keep on looking until the deep reality of the emotion becomes completely clear...

22. From this state, look deeply into the (... the most superficial negative emotion from section 2). Examine what the source of the pain and difficulty of this layer of emotion is... Examine what it is that you really seek in the event that aroused this emotion... Keep on looking until the deep reality of the emotion becomes completely clear...

23. Guide yourself in regard to the event that aroused the emotion within you: What would you do in this event or in similar events from now on? How would you act? How would you respond? ... Finally, encode your body-mind complex to this new form of action: "Align yourself with this new course of action!" ...

24. Express gratitude toward the emotion, which has given you an opportunity to release new energy, to empower your life and to know your true self... Remember that this expanded state is not only your source of healing and insight but also your true home... You can choose to stay in contact with this state within your heart even in your ordinary state of consciousness... For the last time, immerse yourself in this state for renewal and empowerment... Now you can open your eyes slowly and gently.

A Sharing

M., 28 years old, after an initial experience of expanding a negative emotion.

I started the process with expanding *insecurity*. The picture that represented it the most was a date I had had with a girl I had met through the internet. Throughout the date I was filled with a sense of insecurity, accompanied by physical sensations—in the face, shoulders, and lungs. It was a feeling that I could not find myself, that I didn't know how to react or respond, and above all, that I could not be who I am. I was totally dependent on any feedback on her part. I was also feeling angry with myself: "Why am I like this? Why am I so incapable?" This anger only disrupted the communication even more. No intimacy was created and no feeling of warmth, only sheer emptiness.

After the first expansion, I reached the layer of "Missed opportunity." The shape was of lava surging within me, red colored, as if I was drowning in a thick swamp. After the second expansion, I reached the layer of "Anger." This layer felt like an extremely dense energy, a sort of trapped power that only seeks release.

At the third expansion, I suddenly arrived at a plane of "Calm," in which, at last, an unloading of the pressure could take place, almost like sexual orgasm. The entire body softened more and more... I could envision a figure sitting in meditation, and this figure was myself. I felt patience and an ability to contain without limit, to allow space for everything. I felt a silent humor and forgiveness in me.

The fourth expansion led to the plane of "Silence." I felt that this silence included everything in it and that it *was* actually everything. An image of a vast ray of light accompanied it. At the fifth expansion, "Eternity" emerged. This was a particularly exciting space, as it seemed to hold within it all forces of nature and the entire history of mankind. The feeling was of a temple, white and light blue, and it had a subtle smile in it.

Finally, at the sixth expansion, I arrived at a plane that I entitled "God." This state seemed to be my very own self, and I knew in it that, when I am completely realized, it is God since, in reality, there is no divide between me and Him. There was laughter and tears of happiness!

Looking at the problem of insecurity from this state, I could see that the most important thing is to experience and experiment, without fearing the need for a repeat experience, and even to initiate, while agreeing to make mistakes. The whole idea is to dare to be precisely who I am and, all along, to persist until success is achieved. Beyond anything else, I must consider these interactions a sort of game in which there is always the possibility of losing. It's important to spice it up with humor, or some degree of non-seriousness since it is the dramatic position that thwarts the meeting. In general, I must dare to perform changes in my routine, to add, every week, something new and to try out unfamiliar things, because the challenge is far vaster than the dating issue alone—it is all about agreeing to experience life in totality.

8

Subconscious in the White Light Expansion

In contrast to classic psychoanalysis, which was satisfied with making a person functional and neurotic to an "ordinary" extent, the Theory of Subtle Fields reveals a potential for a brand new human existence. This existence is beyond the psychological structure as we know it, beyond both conscious and subconscious and beyond the detectable as well as the hidden layers of thought.

As far as the Theory of Subtle Fields is concerned, the very activity of incessant repetitive thinking as it operates in the brain of contemporary man is a *mental disturbance* that must be removed. A state of mental health is found in a quiet and serene brain that exists without any unnecessary thoughts whatsoever. But how can one achieve such a brain?

In the White Light, the answers to questions, such as "Why are there so many thoughts in my head? Why does thought never stop?" or "How can I attain silence?" lie in two planes of activity:

1. **Abiding in the fields for prolonged periods of time as much as possible**. Such times make the brain go through repeated re-organization, until it learns to align

itself with the high levels of order, harmony and wholeness that characterize the subtle fields.

2. **A thorough disentanglement of the subconscious.** We invest superfluous effort in the attempt to struggle against our thoughts and emotions and to "push them aside," while tending to forget that these shallow thoughts and emotions are nothing but a by-product, a symptom, of a far deeper process: memory connections that give rise to countless completely fabricated needs and wants, which *appear* as conflicted thoughts and emotions. In other words, instead of trying to quiet down our thoughts, we should chop off the roots that cause them to grow over and over again: the memory connections of the subconscious.

To attain a truly silent and simple consciousness—which is, I believe, the next evolutionary stage necessary in our world—we ought to work our way "top down" (by continuously going beyond both conscious and subconscious and by abiding, for prolonged period of time, in the subtle fields) and "bottom up" (by unbinding the memory connections and decisively dismantling the foundations of our subconscious). In the following chapter we shall focus on the second activity, which strives toward our release from the yoke of the subconscious.

What are Memory Connections?

Basically, the "subconscious" can be defined as the hidden driving force of the psyche. Why does the psyche try to attain whatever it is that it tries to attain? Why does it react the way it reacts? What makes it frustrated? What brings it to self-destruction?

We will set aside the intriguing question of whether or not there are positive driving forces beyond the subconscious (when we acknowledge the possibility suggested by the Theory of Subtle Fields, we will become convinced of that), and focus our efforts on cracking the subconscious as it exists in the mental-emotional field.

As already mentioned in the chapters on the Theory of Subtle Fields, we can find the generating factors of our psychological behavior on the wider margins of the mental-emotional field. These factors are, in effect, the deepest reasons for the appearance of compulsive, repetitive and conflictual thoughts and emotions in our mind. It is their presence at the bottom of our consciousness that brings us to the intolerable feeling that our psyche is complicated and embroiled. The generating causes of psychological behavior are referred to in the "White Light method" as—"memory connections."

The central role of the brain is to create the most appropriate conditions for the survival of the organism in time and space. Every experience is examined in the light of this purpose, and as time goes by, two kinds of impressions are accumulated in the brain: the experiences that assure appropriate conditions for survival and the experiences that endanger survival. These impressions turn, eventually, into *imprints*—that is, memories that remain relevant and vital to the continued existence of the individual. The more valuable the experience seems for the sake of the knowledge of survival that is gathered by the brain, the stronger and more influential the imprint becomes. A "positive" imprint is formed when the brain connects a certain experience to an optimal capacity for the organism to survive and thrive, and a "negative" imprint is formed when the brain connects a certain experience to the endangerment of the chances of survival.

Each impression of the brain creates memory connections: connecting a certain experience in life to its implications on the ability to survive. However, not every memory connection will be considered an imprint that brings about, in its turn, a type of psychological disturbance: when a patient in critical condition is rushed into the emergency room, the doctor knows what he must do since a connection between the image before him and a previous knowledge that had proved its efficacy in prior experiences appears in his brain; when we efficiently react to a tangible danger ahead of us while driving on the highway, it is enabled by vital memory connections. The problem begins with the many layers of memory connections that *disguise themselves as necessary* for the survival of the individual and that constitute "symbols" and "signals" of danger that make the brain interpret reality in a distorted way and cause the brain to react with the hectic production of confused emotions and thoughts (for instance, the irrational feeling that "the road is a terrifying, bloody battlefield," or that "every physical ailment is doomed to end in death and agony," is a completely false signal of danger).

This is how, in practice, our psychological structure comes into being: layers of unnecessary memory connections pile up over the necessary layers, until eventually it is no longer possible to tell the difference between the two—a predicament that leads to falsified interpretations of reality and, as a consequence, psychological suffering.

The foundation of the personality as a whole is memory connections. Every experience is registered as a memory in the brain, and as said, if, to the brain, the memory seems highly significant in regard to the chances of survival for the body and mind, the memory turns into an imprint. Further on, as more and more "confirmations" of the imprint are gathered through experiences in life, the imprint begins to assume an "independent status" and gradually becomes a pattern.

A pattern is a far more complex structure than an imprint. Whereas an imprint is only an exceptionally intense and impressive memory connection, a pattern is the imprint in addition to what has formed around it over time—among other things, the way we have adapted ourselves in order to "survive" in conditions that the brain has deemed dangerous for us.

When we experience stage-fright in front of a hundred people who listen politely and respectfully to our lecture, we actually live through unnecessary danger signals of the brain, which are based on a prior experience or even on several prior experiences. The danger signals are, in such a case, no more than a mental disturbance since they distort the vision of reality; they warn us against an event that has already happened, an event that is somewhat similar to whatever is taking place in front of our eyes at that very moment. In such a condition we might become paralyzed since we are completely tense in the face of a danger that never comes. Every question sounds grumbling, every stare seems hostile, and we begin to sweat and have difficulty breathing.

Gradually, in order to cope with this "dangerous" event, we develop certain gestures, certain styles of speech and certain forms of persuasion, and we even show off with exaggerated confidence—in other words, we develop a means of concealment for the imprint to enable us to function in situations that, on the face of it, are not functional for us at all. Hence, a pattern is the imprint along with the coping structures of the body and mind as they have formed and consolidated around it (other structures that are worth mentioning are our more and more complicated psychological reactions to the presence of the pattern in us; reactions such as self-condemnation, depression or anxiety). These structures are similar to the processes of natural selection revealed by Darwin: forms of "mutating" adaptation to certain life conditions for the sake of the continuation of survival and enhancement. When the pattern finally crystallizes in man, that memory connection, which turned into an imprint, becomes a symbol with an existence of its own. This symbol replaces reality, and thus, when a person encounters a certain reality, his entire interpretation of it and reaction to it will only exist in relation to whatever it symbolizes for him. He will not be able to see "what is," and he will not really experience life but rather repeat, over and over again, the experience of his memory connections.

Now, the picture becomes clearer: memories turn into imprints, imprints turn into patterns and, eventually, patterns create the fabric called "personality." The personality, heavily laden with false danger-signals and always driven to divide the entire world into "good" and "bad" according to the imprints of the fabricated survival memory of the brain, is the central reason for the existence of psychological suffering (other reasons, as Viktor Frankl pointed out, might be the absence of contact with the spiritual dimension of existence or disconnection from the sense of meaning). Its display window, a product of functional adaptation, may leave a "good" and "rational" impression, but, in actuality, it is ceaselessly driven by clearly irrational memory connections. It communicates with reality only on the face of it; in actuality, it meets with the representations of reality within its own mind and reacts to them and only to them. Thus, its interpretations, opinions, reactions, tendencies and wishes of the heart are all stained by the past—since the personality is, simply put, a sack of unprocessed memories.

When popular spiritual approaches guide us to be "here and now," our personality is what listens to them—and being "here and now" is the last thing it could ever do. How can a sack of memories recognize the existence of a present, let alone actually be present in it? This means that only a meticulous and maximal purification of the unnecessary memory connections can bring about, naturally and organically, a state of authentic presence in the "here and now." Without such purification, the only thing the personality can do is create some projection of the "here and now" out of its world of symbols and past experiences and, through it, simulate this kind of experience.

Only an extremely profound release of the central memory connections, which are responsible for the formation of our personality, can lead us to the end of psychological suffering and to a genuine silence of the brain. As the brain becomes liberated from these connections, it recognizes the direct reality, in which there are very few reasons, if any, to send warning signals of impending danger to the fabric of body and mind. The brain ceases to interpret each and every moment in reality in a compulsive manner that is based on conscious and, even more so, unconscious memory pictures; the tension comes to an end, and, along with that, there emerges a new and wonderful state of complete listening, which arises at each and every moment along with the "here and now."

When the issue of memory connections is understood to the core, there appears, tightly linked to this understanding, *a complete self-responsibility*, a responsibility that recognizes the fact that our psychological suffering, in its entirety, is created by us, due to distorted listening to reality. Through the raw material of memory connections, we spin psychological suffering around our being, like a spider that entraps itself in its own web. At the same time since nobody is responsible for our suffering but ourselves, we are also the ones who can disentangle the thicket. The ignorant inner activity of the psyche is a hell that we bring about by our very own hands, and therefore whatever troubles us is not a "demon," as some used to claim in ancient times, and certainly not society or our parents, but us and only us.

In actuality, without the hidden tyranny of the memory connections over our perception of reality, we will not find ourselves, even for a single moment, in a state of stress—whatever its form may be: anger, sadness, insult, disappointment, desire and so on. After all, any tension stems from the collision between the memory picture and reality, from the inability to see things as they are and to act in collaboration with them and from deep within them. For this reason, the definition of mental disturbance according to the Theory of Subtle Fields will be the perception of the world through memory connections, whereas a central element of mental health will be authentic presence here and now.

Any copywriter understands, to some extent, the principle of memory connections. The purpose of a commercial is to fix a connection between a certain commodity and an image, a picture, a sensation or an emotion. When the brain ceaselessly takes in a message, according to which a certain drink is the "flavor of life" or the acquisition of a specific car implies "daring to truly live," it is eventually "overpowered" by the load of the habit; from that moment onward, whenever it encounters this product, it will not be able to identify it separate from the message, and in the same breath, whenever the desire to dare to live or to get in touch with the flavor of life stirs within the mind, that commodity, consciously or unconsciously, will appear alongside it. Of course, when it comes to the depths of the subconscious, matters are far more complicated and far less immediate. The symbol has long past moved to the front stage and disconnected from the original memory, which was left buried among heaping, long-forgotten memories, and so it is not as decipherable in the way that one can identify the evident manipulation of an advertiser.

Some time ago, a person came to me for a White Light process. He related to me that he was the owner of a very successful self-employed business. From his words, it was obvious that he had no financial worries at all. Of all things, his main problem was the days in which his business was laden with customers. Whenever a surge of clients flooded the store, he would become so deeply anxious that he would rather earn less—if he could only receive customers in a more moderate and mild way. I chose to perform a process called "The White Light for Hidden Memory" with him, a complex technique that deals with unfamiliar pictures that reside in the depths of our subconscious (elaboration on this matter will follow further on in this chapter). The picture that arose in him was one of a common villager, whom he identified as himself, that one day, while standing at the center of his village, noticed a swarm of robbers gushing from the forest toward the village. In only a few moments, before his astounded eyes, the whole village went up in flames, and plunder and massacre were taking place everywhere he looked. He himself managed to hide, but as he came out from his hiding place, nothing of his previously known world remained.

This ancient picture—which might be derived from the collective subconscious or, alternatively, from the individual subconscious—turned, with the passing of time, into a symbol whose origins were completely forgotten: whenever it saw an erupting swarm of people, the brain sent danger signals to the organism. It made no difference that these people were potential customers—the very image imposed itself on reality, so that his brain met the image inside him and never the plain reality. After this person saw the memory connection and unraveled it in the subtle fields, he freed himself from the burden of memory, and ever since, he has been happy to receive floods of customers entering his store.

Another intriguing example is taken from the world of dream-interpretation. In the framework of the White Light, I met a lecturer who unrolled the following dream for me: he sits in a completely crowded auditorium, and the audience is clearly anticipating his lecture with excitement. However, an old person starts talking about himself and his private life. In doing so, he distracts the audience, and the general excitement dissipates. The lecturer goes to the bathroom. When he returns, he finds out that many people have already left the hall, and others have lost interest in the lecture. On his way back to the lecturer's seat, he sees a pet tiger, dressed in clothes and a harness, jumping around the center of the auditorium. There is complete chaos, and the lecturer goes, again, to the toilet. Eventually, he returns and chooses to run a tape of a successful and famous lecturer and thus wins over the crowd's attention.

When this lecturer underwent the "White Light for Dream Interpretation," he realized that this dream dealt with his incessant attempt to please people in his lectures. He is the pet tiger, a powerful and wild creature giving himself up in order to become loved and accepted. The repeated visits to the bathroom are an expression of anxiety, and he uses the famous lecturer's recording in the dream for the sake of being successfully accepted—while the heavy price of this is letting go of his own voice. He discovered that his hidden will was to be loved by everyone, and for that, he was willing to try any kind of manipulation if only to prevent everyone from leaving his lectures in disappointment. In this condition he, of course, imprisoned and suppressed himself. The dream's message was to release the tiger, to be straightforward, to emanate his true self, to accept that not everyone is going to love him, to stop apologizing, and to stay in his own skill set. At the end of the technique, he corrected the dream. The tiger roared in the hall and drew everyone's attention. He did not "escape" to the bathroom, and when he ran the tape of the other lecturer, he explained to his audience why he could not agree with the words of this popular speaker.

Thanks to this technique—which makes it clear to me again and again that dreams are a screening of private symbols, in which all events and people serve an intra-consciousness understanding and therefore have no objective meaning—we could both learn that the lecturer "spoke" to himself during the dream through a symbolic set of memory connections. The tiger, the visit to the bathroom, and the well-known lecturer were linked to very personal interpretations in his brain: an entire setting that was meant to remind him to dare to be who he really was.

One more interesting demonstration of the principles presented here lies in the world of our fabricated needs and wants, a world that is made of falsified images of happiness that are created entirely by unconscious memory connections. Following the principle according to which the brain perceives reality in relation to the memory connections within it, we can discover how pleasure stems from the alignment of reality with the connections of the brain and how dissatisfaction stems from the inability to adjust reality to inner connections. In addition, following the principle according to which the brain does not react to reality but to its interpretation of reality, we can notice just how much we design our own "fantasy images," or images of happiness, and forcefully try to subjugate another person or another thing to them. This happens very powerfully whenever we fall in love: we are interested in the experience of falling in love, a totally inner experience, and thus we become filled with anger and violence toward the object of our infatuation when it does not live up to our compulsive expectations.

When the brain screens a desire—such as the purchase of a new car—it actually connects the experience to a certain emotional experience, which is what it really yearns for. Man's memory connections have formed a link between some fantasy-image and the satisfaction of a deeper need inside him to get in touch with a hoped-for emotional experience. Due to prior experiences of the same condition, past-experiences that somehow remind him of that condition or even collective images engraved deep inside him, he can no longer distinguish between the emotional experiences of freedom, living boldly and totality, and that car.

It is memory that connects all the senses and generates desire. When we smell a pleasant aroma coming from a nearby bakery, the sense of smell drags along with it the sense of sight, the sense of touch and the sense of taste through the activity of memory, which connects the four and forms something that is interpreted as an experience of complete fulfillment; when we notice a beautiful woman, the sense of sight drags the sense of smell, the sense of taste and the sense of touch toward a fantasy of appropriation of that woman and a libidinous takeover of her. Of course, without the control of memory we can enjoy an aroma without desire and also enjoy a beautiful sight without a compulsive fantasy. There is no need for all those dizzying chain reactions that bind us to circular and repetitive memory.

Now, let us get to know a technique for self-work that is used for the unbinding of the subconscious: "The White Light for Negative Memories."

The White Light for Negative Memories

Simply put, the purpose of the "White Light for Negative Memories" is to move to a certain moment in which an irrational and unnecessary memory connection had been formed—and to unravel it properly through the memory-free subtle fields.

From a certain angle, the subconscious can be defined as layers of unprocessed memories that have been repressed instead of undergoing genuine completion and liberating learning. This means that in those moments in time we lacked sufficient awareness to exhaust and properly digest the experiences (and also to instill meaning and sense in them), and therefore, they have turned into sorts of ghosts that, even though they seem haunting to us, in reality are only attempting to ask our awareness to set them free at last. As long as we are not aware enough, we go on accumulating unprocessed memories. Our fear of pain is so great that in every negative experience we actually "flee" the body and intentionally lose contact with the sensual experience just so we do not have to live through the pain. This is how a trauma comes into being: by our very detachment from the body. In the absence of genuine awareness, we leave an empty space that can be very easily filled with irrational memory connections.

The cure for that is obvious and pretty much stems directly from the "illness:" to untie the memory connections, we should agree to re-experience the event, only this time without escaping; we must agree to be fully present in the body, to instill a new awareness, an awareness that was not there before, and also to acknowledge the fact that, regardless of what took place in the event, we ourselves are completely responsible for the *suffering* created in it, and thus it is in our hands to remove it. Of course, this principle of healing has a far reaching consequence: if we could be present with our entire being each and every moment, we would completely stop creating un-necessary memory connections—the subconscious would not form further, and we would only be left with the need to go back to the moments in our past in which we were not present and perform this vital "amendment" in them.

If this is so, what we require is a genuine, solid and complete awareness, and such awareness is available for us in unimaginable abundance in the subtle fields. Only such an awareness can agree to live through the pain, whatever form it takes, and from it, un-ravel the memory connections and grant new meaning and sense to the suffering of the past. Only such a solid awareness can transmute a horrible trauma into an indispensable experience that has, as all other significant experiences have, contributed to our shaping and further development.

Owing to the subtle fields, an impressively mature willingness awakens in man—to, this time, stay present in the body, to not de-tach at all and to correct and restore the missing awareness at each and every stage. As pointed out in the chapter on Enlightened Psy-chology, when the true self is fully present, it prevents the forma-tion of psychological suffering by its very being. The true self is the master of the brain, and as such, it "makes it clear" to the brain that there is no need at all to form a survival imprint or a repetitive signal of danger; just like a torch of enormous magnitude, it very easily un-veils any kind of memory connection that, in the absence of imme-diate care, has turned into a pattern (from which it is already much harder to get away).

Along with the unbinding of the memory connection, a very healthy process will take place: the imprint will be shaken and will come apart, and, consequently, the structure of the pattern will start to gradually lose its power until it completely dissolves. Then man will be able to see that, even though the present experience in his life somewhat reminds him of a prior experience, it still does not have to be a repetition of the negative experience, and even if a similar negative experience appears in it, this time he can—by the power of insight and awareness—"stand up" to it and remain fully in his body.

I find it important to share a reservation here, too, by pointing out that, in most cases, in order to perfectly untie a memory connection, it is advised to turn to a certified White Light instructor. Such an instructor will possess far more complex techniques, such as "The White Light for Trauma" and "The White Light for Hidden Memory," which are particularly suitable for the disentanglement of connections that distort our experience of reality here and now.

To unravel a certain pattern fully and radically, we ought to acknowledge a possibility that crosses over the limits of our present rational thinking: very often it is not about traumatic experiences from the present lifetime. In this claim I do not mean to decisively side with the familiar notion of reincarnation—yet experience has convinced me that many of our memory connections are simply unexplainable through the old psychological paradigm. For instance, why is it that already in early childhood one tends to interpret a certain experience in one specific way while his friend interprets it completely differently? Why is it that a person experiences fear of flying even though, in his present life, all of his experiences at great heights have been utterly positive?

In the "White Light for Hidden Memory," we expand an irrational connection, which constitutes a mental disturbance for the person, and arrive at a plane of unconscious and unfamiliar memory, which is realized as something highly influential on the man's psyche. Whether these are memories of the collective subconscious or memories of the personal subconscious, it is always revealed, very clearly, that these pictures of memory have a considerable molding influence on the present means of interpretation for the person and on his or her forms of reaction to the current reality. It is amazing to discover, as these pictures unfold, just how creative our brain is—it takes in the pictures through fragments and pieces of sensual and psychological experience, and "recalls" the entire experience whenever it meets a new experience that contains a similar or identical fragment or piece.

Perhaps the most convincing is the fact that the "White Light for Hidden Memory" is the most effective technique for the removal of patterns in the entire method! In my opinion, this stems from the fact that the hidden memory manages to reach the *first* moment in which the memory connection came into being (rather than other moments in which the connection only "re-confirmed" its validity), and in doing so, it chops off the roots of the tangled and thriving tree of the pattern.

In the following technique, you will be able to re-awaken a negative memory, expose through sincere listening the memory connections that have been formed in it (and that, naturally, affect you to this day), and then perform several expansions until you properly settle into the mental-spiritual field. From a completely positive, memory-free expanse, you will be able to simulate "re-entering" the depths of the memory, this time overflowing with liberated awareness, and to work, as much as possible, on untying the irrational connections.

Practice: The Expansion of Negative Memories

1. Close your eyes. Breathe slowly and deeply. Relax more and more with every breath you take... Agree to face this event again within the gentle and protective space of the White Light... Allow this event to fully be, with no judgment or condemnation... Describe the event briefly... Now examine which stages or which points in the event were the most intense and shaky for you... Breathe into those moments. Let them open up within you and reveal their subtle layers to you... Now recall the scene in those moments in as much detail as possible... Now recall the emotions in those moments in as much detail as possible... Now recall the thoughts in those moments in as much detail as possible... Now recall the sensations in those moments in as much detail as possible... What was the state of your body? ... Which area in the body reacts the most to this event? ...

2. Breathe into the (... area in the body from section 1) and keep describing emotions and sensations—don't talk

about your experience from the outside but rather from inside of it, from deep within... What was your level of presence in those moments? How present were you in the body? ... Notice how much you avoided being present, how deeply you resisted this event and how much you tried to avoid it... Examine how your breathing was in those moments... Was there a sense of being a victim, a feeling of "Why does it have to happen to me"? ... Get in touch with the feeling of the victim as it arises within you; feel the resistance to the event and the wish to avoid it...

3. Describe your surroundings and your connection to them during this event... What was the level of your external awareness—were you conscious of everything around you or did the world fade while you were only conscious of the happenings from within? ... Now describe the image of (... the aggressor) - what does he represent in your mind at those moments? ...

4. Describe the initial contact with the event, the very moment in which you realized (... *the most extreme realization, such as "my life will never be the same" or "there's no one to trust in this world")*... Where do you experience it in your body? ... And what does it feel like? ... Let yourself, in this protective space, re-experience the most initial sensations and emotions...

5. What did you experience in your thought? ... Go deeply and examine: What was the belief that made it hard for you to fully face the event at that time? A belief is an expectation that things in life should happen differently... What was your wish, the hidden image of perfection? ...

6. What was the conclusion that you made out of this event? Examine deeply what imprint has been created within you as a result of this event... Keep examining what has been created, as a result of this event, in your body... Keep examining what has been created, as a re-

sult of this event, in your emotions... Keep examining what has been created, as a result of this event, in your thoughts... Keep examining what has been created, as a result of this event, in your actions and behaviors... Keep examining what has been created, as a result of this event, in your general relationship with life... Look for the connection that has been formed within you ever since this event...

7. Now give a general name to the negative experience... Breathe into the (... general name) and feel it deeply. Move into its depth, into its very core. Try to describe it in words. What does it feel like? ... Look for an area in the body deeply connected to it... a shape or an image... a color... a general sensation... a fragrance...

8. Now breathe into the (... general name). Feel it from within. Let it spread wider and deeper and fill your entire body and being. Breathe into the (... image or shape) in the (... area in the body). Breathe and expand, breathe and expand, until it reaches its outermost limit, until it cannot expand anymore. Request: "(... general name), show yourself completely to me!" ...

9. Give a name to the expanded state... Breathe into the (... name of expanded state). Move toward it, into its depth, into its very core. Try to describe it in words. What does it feel like? ... Look for an area in the body deeply connected to this state... a shape or an image... a color... a general sensation... a fragrance...

10. Now breathe into the (... name of expanded state). Feel it from within. Let it spread wider and deeper and fill your entire body and being. Breathe into the (... image or shape) in the (... area in the body). Breathe and expand, breathe and expand, until it reaches its outermost limit, until it cannot expand anymore. Request: "(... name of expanded state), show yourself completely to me!" ...

11. Give a name to the expanded state... Breathe into the (... name of expanded state). Move toward it, into its depth, into its very core. Try to describe it in words. What does it feel like? ... Look for an area in the body deeply connected to this state... a shape or an image... a color... a general sensation... a fragrance...

12. Now breathe into the (... name of expanded state). Feel it from within. Let it spread wider and deeper and fill your entire body and being. Breathe into the (... image or shape) in the (... area in the body). Breathe and expand, breathe and expand, until it reaches its outermost limit, until it cannot expand anymore. Request: "(... name of expanded state), show yourself completely to me!" ...

13. *Keep expanding (sections 11-12) until you move from negative states into positive states. After achieving the first positive state, perform three more expansions. Stop expanding only after you're convinced that you abide in a state in which you are capable of easily overcoming the memory.*

14. From this state of the (... last expanded name), wash your entire being with White Light: body... emotions... thoughts... and your entire being... Wash the (... general name from section 7) from the (... area in the body deeply connected to it in section 7) with White Light... Encode the body-mind complex: "Transform yourself into the light of the (... expanded name)!"

15. From this expanded state of (... expanded name), go through this event again, step by step, but this time agree to experience it fully, with your entire presence... Let the scene arise in your mind again. How do you regard it from this state of (... name of the last expanded state)? ...

16. Through this state of freedom and non-attachment, re-experience the event, but this time—don't avoid it. Let the (... name of the last expanded state from section 15) penetrate those moments; breathe into the (...

area in the body from section 7); say "yes" to the entire situation—and describe what happens then... Stay fully present—and describe what happens then... Agree to breathe—and describe what happens then... Agree to feel the discomfort, the inconvenience, but don't turn the pain into suffering! Describe what happens then... Let go of the feeling that you are a victim. Let go of the thought "why does it have to happen to me?" Describe what happens then... Let go of the way you perceived the (... name of aggressor from section 3)—and describe what happens then... Let go of the (... wish from section 5)—and describe what happens then... Let go of (... the conclusion from section 6). Let go of it from the depths of the (... name of the expanded state from section 15)— and describe what happens then... Let go of the (...imprint from section 6) that has formed in your thought. Describe what happens then...Let go of the (... connection from section 6)—and describe what happens then...

17. How would have you acted in the event? How would have you responded from this state of full presence? ... Now you can see that you mistakenly experienced this event as if it were all against you. Now, instead, observe the event objectively and neutrally, and analyze it properly...

18. Look closely. What was the purpose of this event? What was it meant to teach you? ... How can this event serve you? ... So was it really a negative event or did your perception of it perhaps twist its meaning? ... Form a new connection now, a new conclusion to imprint in your brain... So why have you created this event for your evolution? ... How will you regard this event from now on in your memories? ... Who are you without the negative interpretation of the memory? ... Finally, examine what would happen in the future in an event that might re-awaken similar feelings? ...

19. Remember that this state is not only the source of your healing and liberation but also your true home. Before you open your eyes, choose to keep in contact with this state within your heart even in your ordinary state of consciousness... For the last time, immerse yourself in this state for more liberation and empowerment... Now you may gently and slowly open your eyes...

A Sharing

T., 30 years old, came to the White Light in order to attain balance after years of emotional turmoil that nothing had managed to solve. This is a sharing from after a first experience of the "White Light for Negative Memories"

The negative experience that I chose to work on in the technique was related to a conversation I had had with an old friend at my home when I was seventeen. We had been sitting and discussing the issue of drugs and psychoactive plants, and my friend told me about people who use them and have visions of, and encounters with, invisible entities. As he had been talking, all at once, a question had arisen in me: "Then what is actually real? Is there anything real at all? How can I know that what I see is reality and not my imagination?" I felt compelled to ask this question, as if I had to know the truth, and at that very moment, a horrible surge of heat and fear had risen in me. I started feeling disconnected, as if I were out of touch with reality; as if something had turned itself off inside me. The feeling was that I had lost everything. With all my might, I tried to cling to familiar things, but to no avail. I had thought to myself: "Life ruined me... everything was taken away from me... I am not connected to reality... Nothing can ever get me away from this state." Ever since, throughout all these years, these anxiety attacks have come and gone.

After recalling, in great detail, that conversation, including the thoughts, emotions and sensations I had had during it, I could see, through the "White Light for negative memories," that the belief that had made it hard for me to face the event efficiently, had been that something irreversible had happened, something that would be impossible to ever change. In those moments, due to my lack of presence caused by terrible anxiety, unconscious imprints had been engraved in me - imprints such as: "I cannot know what's real... I have no ability to find the truth within me... No one can help me get away from this state... I am ruined to the core, and there's no possibility for another future... I have to stay away from anything that might shatter my familiar and normal experience..." I then avoided, as much as I could, practices of meditation and relaxation, so as not to encounter the danger within; any treatment I underwent couldn't help, and I did everything in my power to stay in the "normal" state.

After four expansions, during which I lived through the feelings of destabilization and loss, I suddenly arrived at new expanses of presence and illumination. In these expanses, the view of the traumatic event completely changed, as if it were nothing but a picture. I re-lived the experience, and this time, I allowed the surge of heat and fear to pass through my body innocently, without interpretation. I became peaceful and was filled with silence. My own figure became more mature and manly. The negative experience turned into a positive one: as if something about it made me mature and granted me a silent knowing. I saw that only my body had undergone a shake-up. I was quiet in the midst of the storm and needed not resist. My lack of knowing transformed into innocence and openness, and I knew that everything was well, that I needed no one in order to feel well—and therefore, I needed no one in order to get away from this state. I felt ready to go wherever life might lead me, and interestingly, I only felt more like my own true self. I had no thought about what might happen in the future and felt no impending danger.

I realized that if, at that moment, I would have been in a state of total acceptance, completely bright and clear, I could have discovered that this event had been a kind of gift. It's as if life had wanted to show me something during that conversation—my own true self. After more expansions, I reached the state of "Inner light," in which I knew, in a very simple way, that that event was one of the most important and positive events I ever had in my life, a turning point, a point of flowering! Its purpose was awakening; the discovery that, beyond the thin layer of thought, there's never a doubt or a problem. On this plane, I could safely say that I totally trusted life, that the universe is a manifestation of love and that it wants only my greater good. My attitude toward the memory was completely altered, and the change in my interpretation of the memory made me understand that, in the future, if any such event should recur, I would rather let go, out of trust, and allow the whole of it to "go through" me since now I know for certain that the context was always completely positive.

9

Chakras and the
White Light Expansion

There is no question that thought's takeover of the front-stage is a sign of an astonishing evolution that has marked the birth of the human brain. However, this development is accompanied by a heavy price: witty and cunning thought enables man to construct a display window of "normality" and "rationality"—and to push down to the cellars the impulsive and primitive forces that drive him into action. As a result of this ability, a huge gap has been created between the way man thinks of himself and presents himself—the "self-image"—and the reality of his conflicted and chaotic being. This display window is a powerful hindrance to any possible genuine self-transformation, and the only way to break through it into the layers of the subconscious is through direct communication with the irrational elements of man's being.

Freud suggested two forms of communication with the subconscious: dreams and what eventually earned the title of "Freudian slips," an unintentional and careless exposure of irrational memory connections through dialogue with a psychologist. So far we have pointed out several forms of communication that are put into use in the framework of White Light processes:

1. Significant memories from the present lifetime—through which memory connections that influence our mind and body to this day can be revealed;

2. Unnecessary memory connections as they are revealed through moments of tension and friction—any moment in which we internally or externally collide with life as it is may unveil such connections;

3. Fabricated wants and needs;

4. Dreams; and

5. Psychosomatic illnesses and chronic pains.

To this list we now add an excellent way to bypass the display window of the self-image and to directly communicate with impressions that are buried at the depths of our being: the Chakras. Essentially, the seven Chakras (as identified by traditions such as Yoga in Hinduism, Buddhism, the Theosophical Society and the different schools of the "New Age" culture) are seven energy centers that reside in the electromagnetic field and maintain a tight interaction with our body. The literal meaning of "Chakra" is, "Wheel," and indeed, the Chakras operate as efficient energy propellers: first and foremost, their major role is to "attract" the general life force ("Chi" in Chinese or "Prana" in Sanskrit), which is the force that sustains every biological creature, and to conduct it into the body. Each one of the seven Chakras is directly linked to a specific area in the body and leads the life force to the central glands, nets of nerves and organs of that particular area. For example, the sixth and seventh Chakras conduct life force to the pituitary gland and the pineal gland, as well as to the brain as a whole, and the fifth chakra is linked to the throat and the thyroid gland. Mysteriously, these energy centers possess the capacity to "translate" the life force into an actual material nourishment for the physical body. Without this life force, "life" is literally taken away from the body; in its absence, as we observe at the moment of death for any living creature, one cannot even talk about "life," only about the inanimate body.

Aside from their central role as conductors of the life force in the body, the Chakras also serve as storehouses for memory and experience. Each one of them is a storehouse of memories and experiences that are completely unique in nature. In this sense, the seven energy centers are, in effect, the seven layers of the psyche as they have evolved with time, and when examined layer by layer, one can trace in them the process of mankind's evolution, from the dawn of its existence to this day, the hidden structure of the human subconscious and the development of every baby into a mature and integrated human. Naturally, this revelation holds a far reaching implication: through the seven Chakras, we can directly contact our unprocessed and irrational memories and in doing so, totally bypass the veils of thought.

As we listen attentively to each and every Chakra, they reveal to us, slowly but surely, their condition, just as it is—and their condition is, of course, *our own condition, just as it is.* Since each one of them is a particular psychological layer, we can also discover precisely which of the seven layers of our psyche are only partially active.

In my understanding, not all seven Chakras had necessarily existed at the emergence of the first man—at the most, in the beginning the human had possessed one or two energy centers, which were sufficient to maintain such a primitive organism. As the human evolved, different layers of experience, comprehension and the mind started to add up, and in their turn brought about, one era after another, new energy centers. Another theory would be that the human complex had emerged, from the start, with the electromagnetic field that includes the seven chakras, but they had been mostly dormant or nearly inactive—meaning, their full potential remained dormant and awaited man's development (though their broadest spiritual potential is still far from being realized in most humans). The second theory resembles the wondrous principle of a minuscule seed that holds within it the potential of an enormous tree, which is destined to erupt from within it. In this theory, too, we can relate to the fact that, from one era to another, these seven centers have accumulated experience, memory and human understanding.

All of our Chakras are active to some extent. In human beings who have not yet developed their awareness, the Chakras are usually minimally active—operating precisely at the level that is required for the sustenance of the body and the automatic mechanisms of emotion and thought. To this minimal activity is added the load of memories that the Chakras have accumulated and that greatly interfere with the Chakras" capacity to stir optimally. The removal of the load of memories and the growing development of our consciousness are the sole factors that influence the Chakras" ability to operate optimally: the fewer memory connections the Chakra carries, the "healthier" and more filled with life force and balance it becomes—and correspondingly, the mind and body become healthier and more balanced. Furthermore, as we become more and more aware, their dormant spiritual potential is increasingly revealed, like a flower that is opening fully. Ultimately, they turn into our connective points to the five fields.

The great advantage of the Chakras is their surprising accessibility—owing to the fact that, compared with the other components of man's subtle anatomy, they are the closest elements to the physical body. All of humanity shares, with taken-for-granted ease, terms such as, "Don't take things to heart," or, "I have fire in my belly." It is this advantage that enables the technique presented in this chapter, "The White Light for Chakras," to serve as an excellent tool for self-diagnosis and self-balance. Through honestly and directly listening to the Chakras—bottom-up, one after another—we are capable of directly encountering the memory connections that hinder the flow of life force in our body and mind. In this way, we can encounter the unconscious blockages that hinder us, and thanks to the expansion process, we can also "release" them more and more, until a complete transmutation is achieved. Before we get to know the technique, though, we ought to become familiar with the structures of the mind that are linked to each and every Chakra—structures of the mind that altogether, as mentioned above, constitute the picture of our entire being and life.

The Challenge of the First Three Chakras

The three lower Chakras are the foundations of the building of the mind and consciousness as a whole. When they are unstable, unhealthy and unbalanced, the entire building is doomed to collapse whenever it faces stressful life conditions and challenges that it cannot stand up to.

Throughout the years I have often met people, young and old alike, who have expressed explicit interest in the development of their consciousness, and, at the same time, have been deeply frustrated in the face of the fact that all of their spiritual efforts could, at once, "go down the drain" in daily life. They have started asking themselves how one could preserve the expansion of consciousness for prolonged periods of time, and whether this is available for them at all or is reserved only for the fortunate few. The answer to this spiritual frustration lies in the three lower Chakras, and in particular, the base Chakra: as long as we have not thoroughly untied the memory connections in these layers of the psyche, the possibility of stabilizing the consciousness in the subtle fields is not available for us—and this does not stem from a lack of "divine consideration" but rather from an extremely simple principle that any construction worker in this world understands and puts into use.

The memory connections of the three lower Chakras are, in fact, the most primal, and also the most unconscious, forces that drive us into action; they are the prime generators of our feelings, emotions and thoughts. But due to the fact that our concealing thought is not willing to acknowledge their existence, they are repressed into the cellars of consciousness—and naturally, go on influencing our psychological state and all of our behaviors from there. Without a doubt, when Freud regarded the subconscious as a whole gamut of primordial impulses and emotions, he aimed at the three first Chakras.

It is highly important to understand the way the lower Chakras have been repressed instead of receiving the proper liberating treatment. In humanity's distant past, there was no "subconscious" at all. Man had *himself* been all those primordial impulses and emotions

that in today's world have been repressed and turned into the subconscious. For instance, man had *openly* been a territorial and ani-
malistic creature, but gradually, ideas of morality and social order
came into being and repressed these aspects by turning them into
forbidden and illegitimate aspects. In other words, humanity tried
to skip over its genuine state of development through ideas and ide-
als. The outcome of this moral mischief is that man pretends that he
is not driven by impulses but rather by "good" and moral conduct
when, in actuality, a considerable portion of his psychological conditions, actions, and reactions are motivated by primordial forces (that
is why highly intelligent people might be revealed, through a deeper
relationship, as those who are governed in their life by childish and
unprocessed emotions). So, the subconscious is the memory layers
of the primitive being, well-concealed by morality.

Sexuality, power, forcefulness, and the fire of life—and all memory connections that revolve around these primal energies—have
become "forbidden;" thought has learned what is allowed to be expressed in order to be accepted, and accordingly, has suppressed
entire portions of man's being. But these parts cannot just lie there
peacefully as they are buried beneath the land of morality—they are
life forces that must express themselves, and indeed, they express
themselves through neurotic outbursts, dreams and ceaseless conflicts of the psyche against itself. Doubtless, they constitute an enormous part of all those primal emotions that thought faces with utter
helplessness. Quite often, they also succeed in dragging us "down" in
a way that can be referred to as "regressive temptation:" we experience momentary outbursts of the fire of life, craving the simplicity,
power, directness and liberty that lie in the expression of the forces
that reside in our depths.

This finds expression, among other things, in the sexual realm,
through the unbelievable gap between the display window presented by humanity in this field and the amazingly ramified and blatant
pornographic world of the Internet; pornography is the result of the
repression and oppression of the second Chakra—spontaneous, intense and direct sexual urges that morality has forbidden to manifest
in the world. The immediate urges are gradually twisted into fanta-

sies—bound to be expressed in one way or another. They have finally found a haven in the world of thought.

This is indeed a challenging hindrance that stands between us and our ability to create firm roots for ourselves in the three first Chakras: the subconscious is made up of conflicted memory-layers covered by morality, and it is built up layer by layer, in accordance with the evolution of life on the planet; every layer developed from the layer that had preceded it and, at the same time, repressed the former layer through a "morality" of its own. Morality, society's aspiration to achieve order and stable structures in life, represses the previous levels—above all, it represses the three first Chakras. In this way, we find ourselves in a rather uneasy predicament: we cannot evolve as long as we do not integrate the fundamental Chakras into our being, and yet, of all Chakras, they are the hardest for us to directly contact.

If we ever wish to radically develop—a thing that would compel us to become free from the burden of the subconscious—we will have to go through one Chakra after another and generate healing in them by the power of new awareness. Above all, the lower Chakras need an infiltration of the great energy of awareness since, by their very nature, they hold within them the most instinctive survival impressions. Each trauma is engraved, before anything else, in the three first Chakras, and, as already stressed, a trauma is formed when awareness detaches from the body and refuses to return due to fear of pain. An amendment will be, then, to return and to grow upward along the Chakras out of full awareness and infiltrate awareness into all the layers of the psyche that formed and crystallized in an unaware manner. The law is that full presence clears traumas and memory connections, and correspondingly, agreeing to be in the body is a primary condition for the healing of the foundational Chakras.

A Brief Journey along the Seven Chakras

The First Chakra

The first Chakra, located in the perineum (between the anus and the sexual organs) down to the legs and up to the base of the spine, is also referred to as the "Base Chakra"—and not in vain. When its condition is unbalanced, it inevitably radiates this condition toward all others and literally drags everything "down."

The first Chakra is responsible for the survival impressions of the psyche; the direct encounter of the psyche with the forces of life as well as the upheavals of life. From the point of view of an unbalanced first Chakra, life is enormous, cruel and forever shaky, and any change is a kind of enemy. Its most primordial origin is to be found in the struggle for survival of the prehistoric man against the whimsical forces of nature, predators and tribal-territorial wars—a condition in which man did not know when or how his next meal would arrive, and he was forced to move around, moment to moment, in a state of complete tension. This tension is projected on any sort of shake-up in life—divorce, death and moves from one place to another—and this Chakra, in its unbalanced state, holds great resentment toward the fact that life is not stable enough.

The fact of the matter is that the vast majority of humans still "dwell" in the first Chakra and, from it, examine life very suspiciously and with infinite caution. People sanctify the stability of family structures and do whatever they can to preserve balance and repetitive routines in their lives. Those behind communications media earn their bread through incessant, frightening propaganda that aims at the first chakra: they convey the feeling that the world is a dangerous place, a state of uninterrupted horror, and therefore, we must cling, as much as possible, to the tiny boxes of our life's structures.

Primordial fear is the central emotion of the Chakra, which holds all of man's most primal traumas within it: the various encounters with life that proved, beyond a doubt, that life is dangerous and cruel. The memory connections of this Chakra all rest on the grounds of the greatest connection of them all—that at any given moment life might turn over, and that at any given moment a horrible danger might appear from nowhere. The feeling that follows is that everything is against us, and we must, therefore, incessantly defend ourselves - and the best way to defend ourselves is to attempt to create stability and security in life itself and to clutch this fabricated stability and security with all our might.

It is easy to see how stability or instability in this Chakra determines whether our most fundamental experience of life is positive or negative—and it is also easy to derive from that, that, as long as our fundamental experience of life is negative, there is no point at all in discussing the expansion and development of consciousness. No one can feel capable of disconnecting their awareness from the fundamental tension and releasing it toward a wondrous expansion while unconscious danger signals within forewarn that a disaster might befall them in a moment or two!

It is not a coincidence, then, that the central psychosomatic disorders of the unbalanced first Chakra are problems with the spine, back, bones and joints—and it is not a coincidence, either, that the common metaphor for a man who radiates an independent and solid presence is of one who has a "backbone."

Before anything else, the solution required for the unbalanced first Chakra is psychological and functional—not spiritual. In fact, when a feeble first Chakra attempts to cultivate spirituality, it forms what can be referred to as a "fabricated spirituality:" a sophisticated form of escape from life and nothing more (an escape that can also be identified in the psychology of religion, as revealed in fantasies about the "world to come," the "return to heaven" and the "Messianic Age"). In other words, this is not a spirituality at all but rather some form of neurosis—fleeing to a world of delusion that also grants a feeling of superiority and power and, by that, reinforces alienation from others and the entirety of society. The real problem for such a person is his feeling that he is incapable of coping with life's challenges; his feeling of superiority is the last form of power left in him in the face of a frightening and brutal life. Accordingly, if his relations with life are resolved, it is most likely that his "spirituality" would fade, just as illness or psychological disturbance fades away.

It is important to understand that real spirituality is founded on a positive experience of life; it is not a "solution for suffering," since a "solution for suffering" is truly assuming full responsibility for our suffering and being ready to stand up to life's challenges with all our might.

One should understand that the first Chakra in its unbalanced state is also a powerful hindrance to processes of psychological healing. Very easily, it can create a false display that "everything is well with me"—for this reason, it is to blame when even a meticulous Chakra scan ends in a false result of total harmony in body and mind. The wish to avoid any more pain and shake-up, the fear of change in life and the determination to keep the present structures of life at all costs (even if they cause the person enduring suffering!), will quickly gather to stand as a fortified wall against even the most dedicated therapist. Any change, be it internal or external, is a risk that a blocked first Chakra simply cannot take.

The more we unbind the memory connections of the first Chakra, the more it begins to literally liven up. Its ability to authentically "flow" with life, to move without resistance against changes, and to agree to everything, be it pleasure or pain—stems precisely from a new *inner* stability. That is to say, as the individual liberates himself from the hope that the security and stability to which he clings and becomes attach can be found in external life, and as he builds up his backbone, it is revealed that the Chakra's solution is complete self-presence. Such a presence is the unchanging ground that man has sought, and it is capable of facing everything, while never waiting for the blows of life but rather hurrying to graciously welcome changes and even initiate them. Not only that, it does not abandon the body at times of crisis but is, in its entirety, a most profound agreement to life as a whole.

In its awakened spiritual state, the first Chakra communicates with the energic spine of the electromagnetic field—a column that "bisects" the center of the body and that is referred to in the Yogic tradition as the "Sushumna Nadi." It is this column that is capable of conducting the life force, this time in the opposite direction: instead of conducting the life force (the Chi or Prana) of the electromagnetic field downwards, toward the earth, it pulls upward, toward the upper Chakras—a process that enables the progressive spiritual awakening of the entire complex of the body, psyche and consciousness.

The Second Chakra

The second Chakra, located in the area of the sexual organs, lower belly and umbilicus, is the life force Chakra (not surprisingly, it is related to the essences of life force that Chinese medicine referred to as Jing and Ayurvedic medicine, named Ojas). It is already less survival-oriented than the first Chakra and deals more with daring to experience, feel, and sense. Unavoidably, it also deals with the limits of our experiences, emotions and sensations quite a lot—limits marked by morality and social order and by the "permitted" and the "forbidden" standards that were set before us, often for no clear or justified reason, by our parents, teachers, friends, superiors, law-givers and leaders.

For the most part, this Chakra is remarkably active and healthy in our early childhood: we are an eruption of unlimited joie de vivre that seeks to experience, sense and taste everything. We cannot tell what is "allowed" and what is "forbidden," and the world seems like one big playground. However, soon enough, barriers are set before us: for some reason, when we experiment with certain things—such as enjoyably scribbling on the house walls or pulling candies out of an adults" bag—the face of the adult in charge appears in front of us, furiously red, and screams: "Bad boy!" or "This is forbidden!" At such moments, we are astounded to realize that there are things which are forbidden simply because someone decided to forbid their happening—and even if we do not understand why we should let go of them, we simply must let go of them.

Many prohibitions are imposed on the sexual realm in our world—sticky remnants from the ages in which religions controlled the human race. There are also prohibitions in other areas of experience, even some that draw lines for our creativity. With every violation of such a prohibition, be it deliberate or not, we feel guilt and a sense of sin, and we are also often punished. (When memory connections are active in the second Chakra, we become the most terrible punishers of ourselves!) In Hebrew, there is an idiom that can be directly translated to "remorse of the kidneys" (meaning, a pang of regret)—which makes a lot of sense, considering the fact that kidneys are part of the second Chakra. In this way, a vicious circle is created—the wish to experience the forbidden, a violation of a moral law, a punishment for the violation and on and on—and the second Chakra becomes laden with memory connections and is increasingly exhausted. (This is a significant source of various psychosomatic disorders in the sexual system as well as in the formation of compulsive desires and destructive addictions—the life force turns against itself.)

Releasing the memory connections in the second Chakra involves a renewed readiness to experience, feel, and sense—this time without guilt and without a sense of sin. With the exception of situations in which we might cause harm to ourselves or others, a whole new experiential range stretches before us, and, at least to a great extent, life can be perceived, once again, as one big playground. We are allowed to explore our limitations: to dare to feel the intensity of life; to dare to fall in love—and to agree to the possibility of disappointed love (without vowing "I shall never fall in love again!"); to be sexual; and to express creativity (even when it leads to failure in societal terms). The general healing is the feeling that one is "allowed"—and this time, the permission is something that we give ourselves. For this reason, it is, in some respects, the beginning of self-authority.

With the awakening of the dormant spiritual potential of the second Chakra, our aspiration to merge into life gains a new layer—the aspiration to expand our consciousness more and more. Our creative power turns from solely primitive participation in the creative processes of life (in the form of sexual and birth-giving impulses) into the urge to express our gifts and talents out of a communion with life, just as all of nature is a harmonious and natural creative eruption of the cosmos. The awakened second Chakra bestows us with the feeling that we are limitless—not in the sense that we can walk stark naked in the street but rather in the sense of inner freedom—and out of that, we are filled with joie de vivre and the gaiety of a child. Our ability to feel and experience increases, and in fact, for the first time we are capable of knowing the meaning of total experience.

The second Chakra is not only related to the electromagnetic field, but also to the mental-emotional field—as the layers of thought and emotion that deal with creative expression, sexuality, limit-experiences and various longings for experiencing.

The Third Chakra

The third Chakra, located in the area of the upper belly and solar plexus (and, among other things, linked to the digestive system), is the Chakra of individuality. It is very easy to identify the relations between the second Chakra and the third Chakra in regard to the growth processes of children and adolescents: the child is the erupting joy of life, which learns to regulate its way through the different prohibitions of adults, whereas the adolescent is a rebellion against these pressures—a rebellion that aims to mold and consolidate a selfhood of its own. Individuality is, simply put, my experience of self, along with all of my opinions, views and unique ways of experiencing life—against what others say or think about my deeds. For this reason, the most entangled memory connections of this Chakra deal with the reactions of the crowd or the reactions of authorities to my individuality—the crowd that ragingly stones individuals for their views, the arrows of criticism that are thrown when I insist on going my own way, and my ability to remain steadfast in my beliefs in spite of all the pressures.

The consolidation of individuality has one more important aspect: my ability to aspire to the extremes and to fulfill such aspirations; my ability to control and harness myself, for example, to awaken self-discipline within myself in order to direct my life toward my desired destinations, and my ability to act as I wish, without retreating due to being too easy on myself, giving up at the very beginning, shirking the pressures or simply enjoying the convenience of social conformity.

The third Chakra, connected to the mental-emotional field, can also be understood as an emergence of a true self, a presence that is capable of organizing and integrating the countless contradictory voices of emotion and thought into one will. A true self means the ability to know what I want and to realize my will. The lowest level of such a self is the psychological level, referred to as the "ego"—the presence that mediates between urges and impulses, or id, and social orders, or super-ego (it is not a coincidence that the Chakra of individuality is situated above the Chakra of life force; it can lead the life force Chakra to a positive middle point between the socially "forbidden" and what is "allowed" to the inner child). The highest level of the true self is an integration of all parts of the self into a completely simple and harmonious consciousness—the result of a shift to the mental-emotional field.

A balance of the third Chakra is achieved by firmly daring to stand up to social voices and pressures and remain loyal to personal truths, without it turning into a violent and aggressive outburst. Too often, the unbalanced third Chakra reacts with anger and forcefulness, as this is the only way it can feel and experience the power of individuality in the face of others.

The spiritual awakening of the third Chakra leads to the mental-spiritual field, where the discovery of a self beyond thought lies. At the same time, the third Chakra serves as a force that enables us to fulfill our most sublime aspirations and to direct our life toward genuine development, out of self-discipline and a maturity of great profundity. In actuality, the ambitions themselves transform since individuality is no longer focused on its own power but rather on serving life as a whole.

The Fourth Chakra

The fourth Chakra, located in the center of the chest and the upper chest, is also known as the "Heart Chakra." If we go on applying the Chakra continuum to the developmental process of the child and the adolescent, then, at this stage, the young person's maturation is completed through his ability to acknowledge the actual presence of "others" and to engage in mature and responsible relationships with them. One of the most obvious characteristics of a child's nature is narcissism; the feeling that everything revolves around my most immediate wishes and desires; the other exists solely as my servant or supporter, and, in actuality, the other's existence is taken for granted—when the other refuses to focus on me and dares to express contradictory wills, I am filled with rage, insult, frustration and disappointment. Usually, we do not expect a small child, mostly not even a teenager, to acknowledge the realness of the "other" (at the most, we demand teens to comply with the requirements of basic manners and "fake" consideration toward others), but when a teenager grows up and remains a narcissist, he becomes "childish." Therefore, in many respects, the definition of proper psychological growth is the increasing development of our capacity to recognize the "other"—his unique and separated world, his autonomy—and beyond that recognition, to cultivate the skills to initiate mature and engaged contact with this separate autonomy.

As mentioned above, the third Chakra deals with the crystallization of individuality—the selfhood separated from all others. Provided that this Chakra receives appropriate and profound cultivation - that is, provided that individuality does properly crystallize - the next natural stage is to "return to society" and to establish real connections. Indeed, this is the lesson of the Heart Chakra: the relationship between that crystallized "self" and the "others."

In its unbalanced condition, the Heart Chakra reflects a narcissistic state, in which the person ceaselessly experiences childish and victimized emotions in the face of the world. The "I" remains at the center—insulted, heart-broken, hurt, licking its wounds, feeling that everyone is against it, asking to be loved and so on. Above everything else, this narcissistic experience is characterized by the feeling of being an incomplete self, a feeling of a perpetual lack of emotion, which forever depends on the nourishment of others. This self asks, and mostly demands, non-stop attention in the form of affirmation, support, recognition and love, and when it does not gain it (or rather when it *feels* that it does not gain it), it withdraws into itself, insulted and pained (and often it also adds up to self-hatred and self-condemnation—"I'm not good enough and not worthy enough to be loved and to be desirable!").

In the unbalanced state of the Chakra, a person undergoes a genuine maturation, which develops the ability to understand that life does not revolve around him, and that, actually, the question is not how all others and life as a whole can serve him and bestow love, confirmation and a soothing touch on him, but rather how he can serve all others and life itself. The sense of having an incomplete self comes to an end and is superseded by the true self—complete, self-nourished and totally independent, which goes beyond the familiar level of relationships of "receiving" and "giving." In such a state, the sense of being a victim entirely dissolves, and the person will never again lament: "Why does this happen to me of all people? Why do I deserve this?" Above everything else, it is the wholeness of the self that brings about a genuine capacity to love at last, and love, in this context, is the ability to transfer attention, sensitivity and caring from the "self" to the "other."

When the spiritual potential of the Chakra awakens, a most extraordinary experience begins to blossom: there is no longer a relationship between "self" and "other" but rather the "other as my self." This is due to the fact that the sense of the true self, which abides in the heart chakra, increasingly expands—precisely in the way that we perform a process of expansion of consciousness—and the more it expands, the more "others" it includes within it. The well-known Buddhist proclamation that "as long as the world is not liberated and happy in its entirety, I, too, cannot be truly liberated and happy" is an expression of the experience of self as other. In fact, the spiritual potential of this Chakra is so enormous that it is capable of awakening the feeling that one possesses inexhaustible reservoirs of love and giving in the human; the body may become tired, but in the heart, the ability to give more and more exists forever.

In the awakened state of the Chakra, there also emerges what can be regarded as the "knowing heart"—a direct knowledge of the truth and the meaning of life. Contemplating the scientific discovery that there are neurons in the heart itself, which basically implies that it is a sort of "brain," we can certainly assume that this is what many mystics have meant when speaking of the heart that "knows" what the "head" has forgotten.

The Heart Chakra is linked to the mental-emotional field, and in its most realized state, also to the mental-spiritual field (which includes in it, as mentioned, a true self beyond thought and non-causal emotions, which give rise to an authentic type of selflessness) and to the cosmic-soul field.

The Fifth Chakra

The fifth Chakra, located in the base of the throat and the center of throat, is the Chakra of expression and voice. Even if the third Chakra is stable (which implies that we remain loyal to our truth at all costs), and even if the fourth Chakra is stable (that is, we are connected to the deep truth of the heart, feel that our self is complete and without need and, at the same time, are capable of feeling genuine care toward another), there is still the challenge of *expressing* our truth—our beliefs as well as our most profound whisperings of the heart—to the world; allowing ourselves to be revealed as who we truly are. The ability to proclaim our inner truth, or in other words, to externalize it, is the subject of the fifth Chakra.

Without the fifth Chakra, our truth may remain an internal experience. We may know or feel certain things within us, yet the barrier between the excited inner world and the external world may be experienced as a clear and uncrossable borderline. In this sense, the throat Chakra resembles a border between two countries—when the border is open, free and flowing, there is a natural infiltration of information, impressions and people from the exterior into the interior, and the other way around. In other words, our interior is not so "interior;" it naturally flows outwards, without shielding and hiding.

When the throat Chakra is blocked, we tend to think that a direct expression of our beliefs or whisperings of the heart will, necessarily, turn into us throwing hard and offensive feelings at those around us. Such a state of affairs is very likely to happen as long as we repress the flow from within us outwardly to such an extent that the throat chakra accumulates rage that might erupt at any given moment. When we learn to express ourselves naturally—while taking on full responsibility for the fact that, after all, these are our emotions, opinions and views, and therefore they are not in any way an attempt at coercion on our part—we very quickly find the ability to distinguish between that which is truly necessary to reveal externally and that which would be best kept within us.

The throat Chakra is not balanced as long as we are talkative or, alternatively, reticent and reserved. There is no balance in ceaseless emotional expression nor is there balance in keeping all our thoughts and emotions to ourselves. Eventually, we reach the healthy point in which we express that which is essential for those around us to know and understand about us—or, simply, we learn to express that which serves the situation as a whole, rather than merely expressing out of the liberty to express or avoiding out of the erroneous choice to remain uninvolved.

When the dormant spiritual potential of the throat Chakra is aroused, it turns into a loyal servant of the greater truth—the truth that is not "mine" but which is capable of liberating others, expanding their consciousness and making them grow toward wholeness. In this way, the Buddhist concept of "right speech" is realized: the ability of expression is used only for the sake of the constructive and developing force of life, and so, gossip, judgment and the expression of completely insignificant emotions and opinions come to an end.

This Chakra is associated with the mental-emotional field. In its awakened state, it is also associated with the mental-spiritual field and the cosmic-soul field.

The Sixth Chakra

The sixth Chakra, located in the space between the eyebrows and the lower forehead, is also known as the "third eye." This is the Chakra that is responsible for the ability to differentiate between the significant and the insignificant, reality and imagination, truth and falsehood and high and low. Hence, in this sense, the sixth Chakra is the presence that organizes all five Chakras below it and mediates between them—without it, right speech is impossible since we do not have any ability to know what is worthy of expression and what is unworthy of expression (fifth Chakra); without it, it is difficult to know when it is fitting to insist on our individuality (third Chakra) and when it is better to let go of it in favor of focusing on another (fourth Chakra). It is the one responsible for granting the right context and the most appropriate interpretation to things. It is the one in charge of forming integration, the intelligent coordination between all the different components of being. However, as long as it operates minimally, its modes of interpretation will be absolutely controlled by rational and conceptual thinking, and as a result, it will not serve as a presence that organizes all chakras and mediates between them but rather as a tyrant force that suppresses all others.

In its unbalanced state, the sixth Chakra is flooded by an incessant, totally conflicted stream of thoughts, without any ability to identify which ones are the most worthy and sublime and which ones are redundant and even unworthy of attention. One could liken this Chakra to a torch of attention—the moment this torch sheds light on one thought (or emotion) or another, it gains recognition and treatment, and whatever gains treatment, also draws along with it the identification of the entire mind and its unification with it; at any given moment we become the thing to which we choose to give our attention. When the Chakra is unbalanced, its attention moves about without any sense and responsibility, and the outcome is that we are manifested as different people in the morning, at noon and at night—in other words, we become confused and incoherent.

This Chakra is also the one that filters the continuous currents of information that gush toward us from the outside. Which one of them is true and which one of them is false? What is worthy of assimilation and what should be rejected altogether? As long as it is unbalanced it will be unable to reject and push away the irrelevant and the false or, alternatively, to embrace and assimilate things of great significance to the evolution of the entire organism.

In its balanced state, the Chakra enables us to immediately discern the falsified, to listen properly to the situation as a whole, to avoid automatic and childish reactions, to observe without interference and to interpret things as they truly are. It is, in fact, the one responsible for the way in which we understand the most important essences of life—meaning and purpose, self and universe—and when it operates well, our understanding in these matters will be vast and evolved.

When its spiritual potential is aroused, it enables us to get in touch with an objective truth, a truth that lies far beyond the reach of ordinary and limited thought. This truth, which is not some changing idea or opinion, brings forth a new authority to the fabric of body and mind—the authority of supreme knowing that re-aligns all layers of being into a harmony of higher order. This Chakra also allows us to initiate contact with the invisible dimensions of life and the universe and to "see" them, as it were, and for that reason, it is also called the "third eye."

The sixth Chakra is associated with the mental-emotional field. In its awakened state, it is also associated with the mental-spiritual field (visions, intuitions, messages and invisible dimensions) and the cosmic-soul field (objective truths, cosmic laws and orders and the "Master-Plan" of the universe).

The Seventh Chakra

The seventh Chakra, located in the crown of the head (the uppermost tip of the back of the head), is also referred to as the "Crown Chakra." This Chakra is responsible for our communication with the infinite unknown element of life.

Mystics as well as great scientists agree that, fundamentally, the unknowable in the universe is immeasurably greater than the knowable; the universe is 99.99999% an unfathomably profound mystery. Even if the Big Bang Theory is a precise depiction of the annals of the universe, what had been before the universe came into being? And how did the something come out of the nothing, the time come out of the timeless and the visible come out of the invisible? As we start seriously contemplating the mystery, which by its very nature is unknowable, we can tangibly feel its reality beyond any passing thing (among others, our own existence). For this reason, we often refer to it as "*absolute* reality."

The seventh Chakra is the borderline between our experience of a separated self—the experience that we are a somebody with limits and edges, a shape and a name—and the infinity in which the experience of the "I" has no meaning whatsoever. Correspondingly, this Chakra, in its unbalanced state, makes the body and mind cling, with all their might, to the limits of the self-autonomy and push away, as much as possible, the emptiness (or nothingness). Whereas in the first Chakra, which resides far below, there lies a fear of physical death, in the unbalanced seventh Chakra there lies a fear of the psyche's death—the death of the "I." Constant caution against the loss of control and the danger of dissolution—of thought and the known—makes a person distance himself from the state of supreme happiness in which the dividing line between him and the infinite is broken and the self-consciousness completely loses its limitations.

However, it is important to state a reservation here and to stress that one may not necessarily be ripe enough to irreversibly remove this dividing line, and when such a thing does happen to an immature person, this disruption may cause disorientation in time and space and lack of grounding of the most dangerous kind. (This happens occasionally while consuming psychoactive plants and psychedelic drugs.) The mystical process of removing the boundaries of individual experience and merging into infinity should take place in a rather controlled and progressive manner, where, at each and every stage of the evolution of consciousness, one can become more "daring"—and eventually, when this "breakthrough" occurs, it does so on the grounds of balanced and stable lower Chakras (or, in other words, on the basis of an integrated and healthy experience of autonomy). Only a well-established self can merge into the infinite to an extent that will be both irreversible and totally healthy and balanced. Therefore, it is important to experience, again and again, a loss of limitations through the expansion process, while, at the same time, appreciating the necessity of the nervous and cerebral control system that brings us back to the "ordinary state of consciousness" again and again.

Naturally, the Crown Chakra is associated with the infinity of the cosmic-soul field and with the "nothingness" of the pure awareness field.

The perception of the seven Chakras as the seven layers of the psyche holds a tremendously potent insight. Not only do they provide us with the keys to perfect psychological balance and a meticulous transformative process, but they also introduce us to a model of wholesome and total experiences of life and consciousness. After all, we can derive, correspondingly, seven worldviews, seven forms of love, seven types of happiness, and seven challenges of life from the teachings of the seven Chakras; every possible thing can be reflected through the spectrum of this essential knowledge. When we realize that a completely fulfilled life is not achieved through choosing this or that Chakra but that it is, rather, a multi-dimensional experience of them all, from tip to toe, we hold a key to the fulfillment of the broadest potential of man, from his earthly roots to the most sublime heights of his consciousness.

The Expansion of the Chakras

The following technique, which is recommended for daily practice, can serve you on three different levels:

1. For self-diagnosis—through a thorough scan of the seven Chakras you can bypass the display window of thought and examine the foundational state of the seven layers of your psyche.

2. For balance of body and mind—whenever you perform an expansion on each one of the seven Chakras, you will experience an increase of health, peace, and proper energic flow.

3. For the development of consciousness—at the end of each practice you will be able to get in touch with the invaluable experience of self-wholeness and a totally integrated being.

In a White Light process guided by an authorized instructor, this technique is how we examine the flow of Chakras so as to form a precise and gradual therapeutic map. If, for instance, a person comes to a process and diagnoses himself, through the technique, as one whose first, third and fifth chakras are unbalanced, the instructor will choose to devote the initial sessions to the stabilization of the first Chakra (by untying the memory connections in it and also by other means), and only when it is clear beyond a doubt that the Chakra has reached complete balance, will he go on to working his way up toward the higher Chakras. As was already lengthily mentioned here, without foundations, the building will collapse, time after time, even if the intention of both instructor and instructed is genuinely good. Interestingly, often, thorough work on lower Chakras may bring about balance in the upper Chakras for the simple reason that an imbalance in the upper Chakras is quite frequently nothing but the extension of an imbalance in the foundations of the psyche.

Even when we practice this technique by ourselves, it will teach us, again and again, to climb our way from the bottom, from the roots of our being, upward; to never skip a stage or evade one element or another of our psyche. Hence, when self-wholeness is achieved at the end of the process, it is an all-out attainment of our body, psyche and subtle layers of consciousness.

Take this into account: since the Chakras reside in the electromagnetic field, they are subjected to influences of all sorts, not only to the influences of memory connections. After all, the Chakras are responsible for the daily processes that channel Prana into the physical system. As a result, there may be days during which the balance of a few of them will be disrupted for nonpsychological reasons (such as days of sickness), and alternatively, they may function harmoniously in situations of general relaxation and not "give away" whatever is concealed within them. At any rate, the only thing we can do is to listen with honesty, without trying to "compel" the revelation of one emotion and thought or another and also without attempting to "force" a false display of total harmony.

It is possible that on certain days it seems as if the Chakras are free from any imprints, but the truth is that the imprints lie dormant, awaiting the right time to be revealed. Mostly, honest listening can awaken them from their sleep, but sometimes only environmental pressures and extreme challenges in life can tempt them to surface to the conscious level. One way or another, daily listening may certainly spare us from overly intense external blows that come upon us unexpectedly since listening and awareness imply working with patterns way before they are aroused in life itself. The outcome of such a work is the considerable reduction of unnecessary situations in life that are nothing but projections of patterns (for example, tranquility in reaction to situations may prevent totally unnecessary chain reactions)—and, hence, it is an excellent way to "prevent" rather than "cure."

Practice: The Expansion of the Chakras

1. Close your eyes. Breathe slowly and deeply, and relax more and more with every breath you take... We are about to enter a journey along the Chakra system. At each and every stage allow yourself to completely be with the specific chakra and to listen to it in silent awareness until it opens up and reveals its secrets to you...

2. Now focus your attention on the first Chakra area—from the perineum to the base of the spine and toward the legs. Scan the entire area, piece by piece, until you cover the entire perineum and its extensions through your awareness. This scan will enable the first Chakra to awaken and reveal its dormant impressions to you ... Breathe into that area and allow it to slowly reveal the sensations, emotions and thoughts that arise from it. Don't block anything, even if discomfort, pressure or overwhelming feelings of any kind awaken out of this listening...

3. Describe what has awakened in the first Chakra... Breathe into the first Chakra. Move toward it, into its depth, into its very core. Try to describe it in words as it is right now—what does it feel like? ... Look for a shape or image... a color... a general sensation... a fragrance. Give a general name for everything that has awakened...

4. Now breathe into the (... general name). Let it spread wider and deeper. Fill your entire body and being. Breathe into the (... shape or image). Breathe and expand, breathe and expand, until the (... shape or image) reaches its outermost limit, until it cannot expand anymore. Request: "(... general name), show yourself completely to me!" ...

5. Give a name to the expanded state... Move into the (... expanded state). Move into its depth, its very core. Try to describe it in words as it is right now—what does it feel like? ... Look for a shape or image... a color... a general sensation... a fragrance...

6. Now breathe into the (... expanded state). Feel it from within. Let it spread wider and deeper. Fill your entire body and being. Breathe into the (... shape or image). Breathe and expand, breath and expand, until the (... shape or image) reaches its outermost limit, until it cannot expand anymore. Request: "(... expanded state), show yourself completely to me!" ...

7. *Always focus on the area of the specific Chakra. If the expanded state is negative, continue with the process of expansion (sections 5-6). Don't stop until you have reached a clearly positive state in the Chakra. On the other hand, if the initial state of the Chakra was positive, it is enough to expand it only once or twice—toward an even more positive state. In both cases, when you reach a positive state, allow yourself to dwell in it for a minute.*

8. Now focus your attention on the second Chakra area— from the sexual organs to the abdomen and navel. Scan

the entire area, piece by piece, until you cover the entire lower abdomen and sexual organs through your awareness. This scan will enable the second Chakra to awaken and reveal its dormant impressions to you... Breathe into that area and allow it to slowly reveal the sensations, emotions and thoughts that arise from it. Don't block anything, even if discomfort, pressure or overwhelming feelings of any kind awaken out of this listening...

9. Describe what has awakened in the second Chakra... Breathe into the second Chakra. Move toward it, into its depth, into its very core. Try to describe it in words as it is right now—what does it feel like? ... Look for a shape or image... a color... a general sensation... a fragrance... Finally, give a general name for everything that has awakened...

10. Now breathe into the (... general name). Let it spread wider and deeper. Fill your entire body and being. Breathe into the (... shape or image). Breathe and expand, breathe and expand, until the (... shape or image) reaches its outermost limit, until it cannot expand anymore. Request: "(... general name), show yourself completely to me!" ...

11. Give a name to the expanded state... Move into the (... expanded state). Move into its depth, into its very core. Try to describe it in words as it is right now—what does it feel like? ... Look for a shape or image... a color... a general sensation... a fragrance...

12. Now breathe into the (... expanded state). Feel it from within. Let it spread wider and deeper. Fill your entire body and being. Breathe into the (... shape or image). Breathe and expand, breath and expand, until the (... shape or image) reaches its outermost limit, until it cannot expand anymore. Request: "(... expanded state), show yourself completely to me!" ...

13. *If desired, continue with the process of expansion (sections 11-12).*

14. Now focus your attention on the third Chakra area—from the upper belly to the solar plexus. Scan the entire area, piece by piece, until you cover the entire upper belly through your awareness. This scan will enable the third Chakra to awaken and reveal its dormant impressions to you... Breathe into that area and allow it to slowly reveal the sensations, emotions and thoughts that arise from it. Don't block anything, even if discomfort, pressure or overwhelming feelings of any kind awaken out of this listening...

15. Describe what has awakened in the third chakra... Breathe into the third Chakra. Move toward it, into its depth, into its very core. Try to describe it in words as it is right now—what does it feel like? ... Look for a shape or image... a color... a general sensation... a fragrance... Finally, give a general name for everything that has awakened...

16. Now breathe into the (... general name). Let it spread wider and deeper. Fill your entire body and being. Breathe into the (... shape or image). Breathe and expand, breathe and expand, until the (... shape or image) reaches its outermost limit, until it cannot expand anymore. Request: "(... general name), show yourself completely to me!" ...

17. Give a name to the expanded state... Move into the (... expanded state). Move into its depth, into its very core. Try to describe it in words as it is right now—what does it feel like? ... Look for a shape or image... a color... a general sensation... a fragrance...

18. Now breathe into the (... expanded state). Feel it from within. Let it spread wider and deeper. Fill your en-

177

tire body and being. Breathe into the (... shape or image). Breathe and expand, breath and expand, until the (... shape or image) reaches its outermost limit, until it cannot expand anymore. Request: "(... expanded state), show yourself completely to me!" ...

19. *If desired, continue with the process of expansion (sections 17-18).*

20. Now focus your attention on the fourth Chakra area—from the center of the chest to the upper chest. Scan the entire area, piece by piece, until you cover the chest through your awareness. This scan will enable the fourth Chakra to awaken and reveal its dormant impressions to you... Breathe into that area and allow it to slowly reveal the sensations, emotions and thoughts that arise from it. Don't block anything, even if discomfort, pressure or overwhelming feelings of any kind awaken out of this listening...

21. Describe what has awakened in the fourth Chakra... Breathe into the fourth Chakra. Move toward it, into its depth, into its very core. Try to describe it in words as it is right now—what does it feel like? ... Look for a shape or image... a color... a general sensation... a fragrance... Finally, give a general name for everything that has awakened...

22. Now breathe into the (... general name). Let it spread wider and deeper. Fill your entire body and being. Breathe into the (... shape or image). Breathe and expand, breathe and expand, until the (... shape or image) reaches its outermost limit, until it cannot expand anymore. Request: "(... general name), show yourself completely to me!" ...

23. Give a name to the expanded state... Move into the (... expanded state). Move into its depth, into its very core.

Try to describe it in words as it is right now—what does it feel like? ... Look for a shape or image... a color... a general sensation... a fragrance...

24. Now breathe into the (... expanded state). Feel it from within. Let it spread wider and deeper. Fill your entire body and being. Breathe into the (... shape or image). Breathe and expand, breath and expand, until the (... shape or image) reaches its outermost limit, until it cannot expand anymore. Request: "(... expanded state), show yourself completely to me!" ...

25. *If desired, continue with the process of expansion (sections 23-24).*

26. Now focus your attention on the fifth Chakra area—from the base of the throat to the center of the throat. Scan the entire area, piece by piece, until you cover the entire throat through your awareness. This scan will enable the fifth Chakra to awaken and reveal its dormant impressions to you... Breathe into that area and allow it to slowly reveal the sensations, emotions and thoughts that arise from it. Don't block anything, even if discomfort, pressure or overwhelming feelings of any kind awaken out of this listening...

27. Describe what has awakened in the fifth Chakra... Breathe into the fifth Chakra. Move toward it, into its depth, into its very core. Try to describe it in words as it is right now—what does it feel like? ... Look for a shape or image... a color... a general sensation... a fragrance... Finally, give a general name for everything that has awakened...

28. Now breathe into the (... general name). Let it spread wider and deeper. Fill your entire body and being. Breathe into the (... shape or image). Breathe and expand, breathe and expand, until the (... shape or image)

reaches its outermost limit, until it cannot expand anymore. Request: "(... general name), show yourself completely to me!" ...

29. Give a name to the expanded state... Move into the (...
expanded state). Move into its depth, its very core. Try to
describe it in words as it is right now—what does it feel
like? ... Look for a shape or image... a color... a general
sensation... a fragrance...

30. Now breathe into the (... expanded state). Feel it from
within. Let it spread wider and deeper. Fill your entire body and being. Breathe into the (... shape or image). Breathe and expand, breath and expand, until the
(... shape or image) reaches its outermost limit, until it
cannot expand anymore. Request: "(... expanded state),
show yourself completely to me!" ...

31. *If desired, continue with the process of expansion (sections 29-30).*

32. Now focus your attention on the sixth Chakra area—
from the center of the eyebrows to the lower forehead.
Scan the entire area, piece by piece, until you cover the
lower forehead through your awareness. This scan will
enable the sixth Chakra to awaken and reveal its dormant impressions to you ... Breathe into that area and
allow it to slowly reveal the sensations, emotions and
thoughts that arise from it. Don't block anything, even
if discomfort, pressure or overwhelming feelings of any
kind awaken out of this listening...

33. Describe what has awakened in the sixth Chakra...
Breathe into the sixth Chakra. Move toward it, into its
depth, into its very core. Try to describe it in words as it
is right now—what does it feel like? ... Look for a shape
or image... a color... a general sensation... a fragrance...

Finally, give a general name for everything that has awakened...

34. Now breathe into the (... general name). Let it spread wider and deeper. Fill your entire body and being. Breathe into the (... shape or image). Breathe and expand, breathe and expand, until the (... shape or image) reaches its outermost limit, until it cannot expand anymore. Request: "(... general name), show yourself completely to me!" ...

35. Give a name to the expanded state... Move into the (... expanded state). Move into its depth, its very core. Try to describe it in words as it is right now—what does it feel like? ... Look for a shape or image... a color... a general sensation... a fragrance...

36. Now breathe into the (... expanded state). Feel it from within. Let it spread wider and deeper. Fill your entire body and being. Breathe into the (... shape or image). Breathe and expand, breath and expand, until the (... shape or image) reaches its outermost limit, until it cannot expand anymore. Request: "(... expanded state), show yourself completely to me!" ...

37. *If desired, continue with the process of expansion (sections 35-36).*

38. Now focus your attention on the seventh Chakra area—the crown of the head. Scan the entire area, piece by piece, until you cover the entire vertex through your awareness. This scan will enable the seventh Chakra to awaken and reveal its dormant impressions to you ... Breathe into that area and allow it to slowly reveal the sensations, emotions and thoughts that arise from it. Don't block anything, even if discomfort, pressure or overwhelming feelings of any kind awaken out of this listening...

39. Describe what has awakened in the seventh Chakra... Breathe into the seventh Chakra. Move toward it, into

its depth, into its very core. Try to describe it in words as it is right now—what does it feel like? ... Look for a shape or image... a color... a general sensation... a fragrance... Finally, give a general name for everything that has awakened...

40. Now breathe into the (... general name). Let it spread wider and deeper. Fill your entire body and being. Breathe into the (... shape or image). Breathe and expand, breathe and expand, until the (... shape or image) reaches its outermost limit, until it cannot expand anymore. Request: "(... general name), show yourself completely to me!" ...

41. Give a name to the expanded state... Move into the (... expanded state). Move into its depth, its very core. Try to describe it in words as it is right now—what does it feel like? ... Look for a shape or image... a color... a general sensation... a fragrance...

42. Now breathe into the (... expanded state). Feel it from within. Let it spread wider and deeper. Fill your entire body and being. Breathe into the (... shape or image). Breathe and expand, breath and expand, until the (... shape or image) reaches its outermost limit, until it cannot expand anymore. Request: "(... expanded state), show yourself completely to me!" ...

43. *If desired, continue with the process of expansion (sections 41-42).*

44. Now focus your awareness on the entire continuum of the Chakras, which creates a central column that crosses the body from the perineum to the crown of the head. Breathe into the central column. Move into its depth, into its very core. Try to describe it in words as it is right now—What does it feel like? ... Look for a shape or image... a color... a general sensation... a fragrance... Finally, give it a general name...

45. Now breathe into the (... general name). Let it spread wider and deeper. Fill your entire body and being. Breathe into the (... shape or image). Breathe and expand, breathe and expand, until the (... shape or image) reaches its outermost limit, until it cannot expand anymore. Request: "(... general name), show yourself completely to me!" ...

46. Give a name to the expanded state... Move into the (... expanded state). Move into its depth, into its very core. Try to describe it in words. What does it feel like? ... How do you perceive life from this awakened state? ... Use the White Light to wash your body... emotions... and thoughts... encode the body-mind complex: "transform yourself into the light of (... the new expanded state)!" ...

47. *Dwell in this purified and balanced state of the Chakras for as long as you would like...* Remember that this state is not only the source of your healing and liberation but also your true home. Before you open your eyes, you can choose to remain in contact with this state in your heart even in your ordinary state of consciousness. For the last time, immerse yourself in this state to deepen the liberation and purification... Now you may slowly and gently open your eyes.

Note: The technique maintains its effectiveness even if you choose to stop after the lower chakras or prefer to focus from time to time on one specific chakra, in which case you can go on expanding it to your heart's content.

10

Creative Action in Your Personal Life

So far, we have dedicated a great deal of attention to the contribution of the fields and the expansion process on our psychological and internal dimension. In different ways, we have demonstrated how a new kind of "Enlightened Therapy" comes into being out of the tremendous liberating potential of the subtle fields. However, a therapeutic process, as deep-going as it may be, is not enough to fill a person with happiness and a sense of meaning and purpose. Actually, without creativity, meaning our conscious and full participation in the process of life, and without a profound sense of meaning, we may find ourselves terribly suffering and frustrated. Undoubtedly, the disentanglement of the memory connections is powerful enough to remove the blockages of consciousness that hinder a direct and liberated action in life itself, yet it cannot help us in defining the exact nature of the most accurate and harmonious action or in outlining an actual course for our life.

Fortunately, the fields of consciousness do not only provide a tremendous relief from the psychological dimension but also serve as spaces of great potential for the re-creation of ourselves and each and every field of our lives—for the simple reason that the fields of consciousness are the source of the deepest creativity and sense of meaning available for man. As soon as a person experiences a direct interaction of his brain with one of the three subtlest fields—the third, fourth and fifth fields—the brain becomes at once silent, vibrating with life, holistic and free from the unnecessary activity of memory. In such a state the brain becomes a sort of receptor or, to be more precise, a co-creator of the fields of consciousness. In other words, the *center* of activity is shifted to the vast consciousness and leaves the brain.

When one or more of the three subtle fields spreads out, primarily the third and fourth fields, they constitute an inexhaustible source of visions, non-linear intelligence, opportunities for creativity, and insights into our role in the cosmic puzzle. Since our five fields of consciousness are, in many respects, five hidden senses that are capable of contacting the infinite fields of the universe, they possess the power to draw wisdom, clarity and knowledge not only from within themselves but also from the immeasurably vast and creative cosmos.

The third, mental-spiritual field is a remarkable spring of visions and revelations, messages from our higher self, authentic intuitions, and groundbreaking insights and ideas. It seems like more than a few scientists, as well as many great artists, have drawn their highly impressive creative bursts from this field, which often awakens out of the exhaustion of the limits of familiar thought and the determined aspiration to transcend thought in order to discover something completely new. Albert Einstein's reports of the ways in which he developed his theories were, more than anything else, depictions of an ecstatic mystical state. The American Biochemist and 1993 chemistry Nobel Prize winner, Kary Mullis, claimed that his innovations in the field of DNA stemmed directly from his LSD experiences—a very interesting claim since psychoactive plants and psychedelic drugs often enable us to temporarily settle into the third field. J.K. Rowling, the author of the Harry Potter books series, relates that the vision of the entire series burst forth into her mind while on a crowded train: "The idea for Harry suddenly *fell into* my head. I simply sat and thought for four hours, and all the details *bubbled up* in my brain." (The markings are mine—S.T.) The young composer Jay Greenberg, born in 1991, has been hailed as the "New Mozart" after he started, in his early teens, to write down complete, immaculate symphonies in only a few hours. When asked about the creative process, he said that he actually never thinks of the symphony or plans it beforehand but rather simply hears it in its entirety, from beginning to end, and all that is left for him is to write it down. He made it clear that he feels no ability to alter whatever he hears. These are, of course, only four random examples.

The fourth, cosmic-soul field contains all orders of creation and cosmic law, and great masters along history, such as the Kabbalists in Judaism and Yogis in Hinduism, derived from it the highly complex hidden knowledge of universal structures and the ways we ourselves can influence them. The "Master plan" of the universe lies in this field—the "first cause" of the world, its logic and developmental direction—and correspondingly, our individual share in the great puzzle lies there too. This means that penetrating this subtle field can grant us the ability to reveal, even if only a small portion of it, the meaning and purpose for which we came into being, both as humanity and as individuals within it—in other words, we may discover the objective sense of our existence in it. On the other hand, this is also the field of the infinite potential of the cosmos, an enormous space of creative freedom since, at its depths, every idea and thought-form is "born," and therefore, one can say that, in it, we discover the aspect of the creator within us, the one that can take an active and conscious part in the endeavor of creation. While the third field is an excellent source of creativity for us, in the fourth field we can realize ourselves as a *creating force*.

The fifth, pure awareness field is like the meditation of the entire cosmos; a meditation on the empty space of the primordial universal being even prior to the creation of the universe. Even though in the field of pure awareness, unlike the third and fourth fields, which are teeming with life, there is no creative activity, it still serves as a vital and forever-supportive ground on which we take active part in the world and to which we can also return at the end of each such action.

Nowadays, as members of the free world, we are born into what could be thought of as a "vacant space." This vacant space is the outcome of two important processes: the first is the weakening of traditions and "isms," which leave us without direction and purposes "bigger" than us (along with an increasing emphasis on "self-fulfillment"), and the second is the improvement of the quality of life, which leaves more and more free time on our hands, and with it—boredom and puzzlement in regard to the meaning of our lives.

When nobody tells us what we should do and nothing pre-directs our choices, and, in addition, when we are free from the survival struggle for our next meal, we find ourselves, inevitably, in a more or less conscious state of anxiety or existential neurosis. We must invent ourselves in one way or another—know what we "want" and even "who" we want to be! We are required to pour meaning and purpose into our life with our very own hands, whereas we do not know *why we are alive* at all. As Viktor Frankl maintains in his book, referenced earlier, *Man's Search for Meaning*, the contemporary man must understand that the question, "What is the meaning of life?" is now directed toward him and no longer toward the great life, that it is actually "life asking him."

When we examine this tremendous challenge for man at our present stage, we can definitely assume that the number one cause for unhappiness is not psychological disturbance of any kind but simply a lack of direction, meaning, and purpose in life, i.e. an emptiness that pervades the entire free world. If anything, this emptiness is, in itself, a fertile ground for the formation of many neuroses that could have been solved by themselves with the appearance of a clear knowledge of purpose.

The great beauty of the tangible existence of subtle fields beyond the brain is the fact that it is like a constant invitation to the discovery of a much vaster human potential, one that exceeds the limits of our familiar thought and perception. As our consciousness expands, we can reexamine choices in our lives without the control of fear and other destructive emotions; we can discover how to fulfill our skills and even how to reveal new skills and abilities within us; we can learn how to realize the deepest potential that lies dormant at our depths, a potential that, in many respects, stems from the meaning and direction of the universe as a whole; above everything, we have the capacity to clearly know what is really important and what is negligible in our life; which parts in our being cry out to be revealed and which parts we must leave behind—and we also have the ability to gradually take on the responsibility required for this immensely profound fulfillment of our essence.

The vacant space that increasingly grows with time can only be wisely filled by a very wide consciousness, which is associated with fearlessness and silence and also with truly sublime values and meaning. Turning with such a far-reaching challenge to a limited brain, which is conditioned only to memory connections, is a rather cruel demand; it can only make sense when a wholesome and integrated consciousness faces it. Deep at heart, many of us suspect, quite justifiably, that the truly important answers lie within us, but the great advantage of the White Light does not only lie in the fact that it turns each and every question inwards, toward our depths, but also in the fact that it provides us with the ability to develop a consciousness that befits the required challenge. Whether we like it or not, at this age, we turn into the exclusive creating authority of our lives, and in the subtle fields, this state of affairs can transform into a thrilling potential and an inconceivable creative opportunity—before anything else, the opportunity to create our greatest piece of art: our very selves.

Not every problem of a psychic nature can or should be resolved through therapy or an internal and emotional understanding. Very often, the source of the psychological problem lies in erroneous choices, a lifestyle that is not tuned to our unique structure or a disconnection from a sense of meaning. Sometimes a depressed person should leave his partner and not necessarily treat his "depression;" when he does leave, the depression will vanish as if it had never been. The almost-compulsive tendency of so many of us toward performing self-psychoanalysis makes us forget that there are many ailments that stem from problems of universal imbalance, collective psychological disturbances, as well as vast spiritual and existential problems. This fact demands a highly refined state of listening, otherwise we might find ourselves obstructing and repressing totally different wishes of the heart, such as the completely genuine need for meaning or for accurate action and sometimes also for a change of life structures.

A significant part of the healing of our psyche is finding a meaning or purpose that fulfills the utmost positive potential held within the structure of our body and mind. Another part of the healing is knowing what we ought to choose and how we should act in important junctions in our life. As already mentioned since no one can tell us what a right action is, we must create such an action *moment by moment*. There is no fixed set of laws, and actions are not categorically right since at each and every stage a specific action is required - and even a specific worldview that we should temporarily adopt. The rules of "morality" become more and more vague in time, and the very definition of "right" and "wrong" no longer seems fixed and absolute, and this means that we should find spaces within ourselves that can stand up to the incredible mission of defining "right" and "wrong" at each and every stage; the mission of shaping our lives in such a flexible manner that we do not hold on to pre-determined notions concerning the worthy way of living anymore but rather adapt a rare skill of listening for ourselves, which meets, here and now, the situation as a whole. Such a skill of listening evolves, pretty easily, in the subtle fields.

The True Creativity

Creativity is not only writing a book, setting up a show in the theater, or composing a spectacular symphony. Before anything else, creativity is the way in which our consciousness encounters reality moment by moment and co-operates with it. From this follows that our actions and reactions should become creative—and herein lies the answer to the question "What is a right action for the contemporary man who is free from religious, national and ideological morality?" A right action is, simply, a creative action.

Except for momentary bursts, a creative action is not an actual possibility within the range of our current brain. This brain, loaded with unnecessary memory connections and conditioned to frag-mentary and linear thinking, can only raise from within it what it already knows and "remembers." Eventually, whether in the artistic act or in any other sort of action, it will become "locked" on one particular structure of thought and behavior that it discovered to be efficient, and it will simply repeat it over and over again. This contrasts the very creative dynamic, which is the perpetual striving toward the breakthrough of the structure out of the wish to discover a new, more complex, intelligent and aware structure. The creative dynamic cannot tolerate fixed structures—its only wish is to form new structures. But in order to tune ourselves in to such a dynamic, we must disengage from our present brain and cross the line toward the subtle fields of consciousness.

A conditioned and limited consciousness cannot maintain the wild spirit of creativity for a long time. Again, we should remember that, as long as the brain is disconnected from the fields, its function is only to identify, for the sake of the organism, the repetitive actions and reactions that it can adapt for itself in order to survive in the best way possible. From this we can learn that the present brain has no interest in the constant creative state and even no need for it. As far as our present brain is concerned, there is nothing more exhausting and less efficient than maintaining a perpetual alertness in which appropriate action comes into being out of completely listening to the moment. Perhaps the only thing that might wake it up from its deadlock and fixation is a state in which the organism of whom it is in charge sounds an outcry of despair due to the fact that, after all, the end-result of all the self-preserving efforts is conflict and chaos, misery and painful inner contradiction.

The third and fourth fields adapt our brain to the perpetual cre-ative state. Obviously, we may use them in order to derive insight concerning a certain situation in life, yet it is in their power to do much more than that: the more we experience them, the more they quiet down the activity of inherently uncreative thought and con-nect the brain to spaces whose most fundamental nature is creativity itself. Such a reversal does not occur overnight, and it demands cul-tivation; above anything else, it demands the adaptation to activity from the subtle fields, but with the passing of time, we acquire the capacity to create our life—its "now" as well as its future. The third and fourth fields provide us with the perfect conditions for creative action:

1. *A quiet yet active brain.* The center of the brain's activity ceases to be memory-based, repetitive routes of thought and shifts to a state of listening or pure and holistic perception, without immediate conceptual interpretation or comparison to something familiar, and also without distorting emotions. Although this state might be pictured in the mind as a passive position of the brain, listening is not static; it is more like a "total wakefulness," vibrating with life, in which only the neurotic doing of thought ceases to exist. I call it "an active silence." In this silence there are no conclusions and interpretations but rather the constant use of the tremendous power of questions. A question, when properly held within our mind, concentrates our entire cerebral effort into a genuine attempt to understand that which *we do not yet know.* The very state of questioning is a state of openness and totality of listening. In this active silence, the brain does not rush toward answering the question—in many respects, it becomes itself a question mark, wanting to know, but it never limits beforehand whatever may be revealed before the mind's eye. This state naturally leads to section 2.

2. *Insight out of listening.* On the grounds of "active silence," a totally new mental activity begins to take place. The moment the brain is quiet to such a great extent, owing to its communication with the subtle fields that align it with a state of existence beyond thought, a different form of perception and understanding awakens in it. In this form, the familiar linearity of our thinking—the logic of an argument that follows from another argument, as well as the "for or against" position and the attempt to reach a conclusion through mental effort—is absent.

"Insight" takes the place of linearity: a direct seeing of the thing, without any effort or logical structuring. This seeing is never a mental understanding alone—it includes emotion and the body as well as the fields of consciousness; its authenticity echoes throughout our entire being; we simply "know" it is true. An insight, by its very nature, is always liberating, always developing, always constructive—it is like a thread thrown in our direction from the unknown of life, a thread that if we only follow it, will lead us to our next step, the next evolutionary level of our consciousness and our life. As mentioned, an insight is an activity received by the brain from the third, mental-spiritual field, and in fact, through it, every scientist and every artist has attained their non-linear understandings and visions; now the White Light allows a steady and systematic method to reaching such insights.

3. *The sense that everything is possible.* True creativity cannot be enabled as long as there is a sense of problem and barrier, and on the other hand, it is infinite as soon as there is no sense of problem and barrier. At the level of creative action, one can see this easily: when we are stressed and worried, our ability to solve a problem in an unexpected way is nearly non-existent, and from this follows that if we wish to properly tackle problems in our life, we ought to start with the real problem, which is the lack of harmony in our consciousness. A creative action is always an action of positivity, changing reality without a conflict (usually it seems to us that we want to change reality only as long as we keep "arguing" with it, but the truth is that when we stop arguing with reality, we can finally, for the first time, *create* it). In the fields of artistic or scientific creativity, the state referred to as "creative block" is nothing but a thicket of thoughts and emotions from which we need to get away, moving instead toward open fields in which this thicket cannot possibly exist— and so at once our creative block will be lifted. If we wish

to feel the power of the fields to generate the feeling that everything is possible for a moment, we simply need to ask ourselves at each and every point of indecision and block: "If I had no limitation whatsoever, what would I have chosen to do?" For the brain that is linked with the third and fourth fields, there is nothing that cannot be solved; there is no dead-end since the very feeling that there is a dead- end can stem only from conflictual thought.

4. *Seeing processes from bird's eye view.* Being fragmentary by nature, thought can only see one small part of the picture at any given moment. In its very essence, it focuses, rather than expands, out of its mistaken survival assumption that only by turning intense attention toward an object can one attain the desired understanding of it. In stark contrast to that, the subtle fields expand consciousness to such an extent that it can see anything it wishes to create (be it a creative action or an act of art) *in its entirety*. It is all a matter of proportions: when consciousness is wide enough, the object appears while abiding in a vibrating and infinite space in which everything is possible. In such a way, it is very easy to identify the next step of development that we wish to take for our object of creation.

5. *Tuning in to the "Universal Will."* Our most sublime creativity is revealed at the perfect meeting point between optimal self-fulfillment—the utmost realization of the potential held within us—and service for the sake of the whole. In other words, we are fully realized when we discover how to harness the best in us for the sake of all others. No wonder: the universe perceives us all as parts in a wholesome puzzle, and in its wisdom, it encodes each and every one of us with a certain potential, which, in its full blossoming, is destined to support the general blossoming. That is why there is no point in cultivating

moral ideas such as "selflessness" or "helping our fellow-man." If we take on full responsibility for the mission of fulfilling the utmost potential in us (hidden deep within the third and fourth fields), it will become clear to us that it is inseparably intertwined with us turning ourselves into a gift to all others, anyway. When we fulfill ourselves only minimally or partially, our contribution for the whole will also be small. This is a universal law: being completely myself means, at the same time, coming out of myself completely. Another law is that true creativity and service for the sake of the whole are always discovered to be two sides of the same coin.

As mentioned, creative action from the fields is not something we are accustomed to, and for this reason, we must first get used to prolonged immersion in the fields, not expect that extraordinary ideas and insights will appear in us at once. At the first stage, our brain will be so stunned by the ever-deepening enlightened states that it will barely be able to mutter a few broken sentences, but the more it becomes accustomed to the state, the more that miracle will take place in us, and we will discover for ourselves that silence can speak and act, and hence, that it is possible to unite activity and enlightenment and, in effect, to live enlightenment with eyes wide open.

Of all people, it is the experienced meditators who sometimes find it hard in their initial encounters with the White Light to accept the possibility that one could speak and act out of silence. Indeed, sometimes it seems that our meditation is so deeply rooted that the link to the "outer world" is cut off completely and there is no point talking or contemplating life. Yet, we should understand that behind this insistence to stay in the meditative state often hides a fundamental hatred of life—we tend to use the expanded states as escapes from life, instead of striving for action out of these vast states. To the extent that this is true, we ought to resolve this unprocessed and well-concealed resistance of the lower Chakras, so we may discover that the fields of consciousness are not meant only for relief and release but rather, are, in a sense, the most sought-after practical keys to changing our life and the entire world.

The following technique is meant to provide you with the ability to realize creative action. This is achieved through The Expansion of a Question to which you seek a solution. You are welcome to raise a question that either troubles or fascinates you, and then to take it on a journey of repeated expansions, while, along the way, deepening your communication with it more and more. After a few expansions the question itself will dissolve, but in spite of your feeling that it is no longer relevant, perform one more expansion. With the additional expansion you will reach the depths of the third field, a state of being in which everything seems resolved and all is possible. From this state you will be able to allow further contemplation of the question to your heart's content.

It is worth mentioning again that this self-work technique can support us on a daily basis in our attempts to define our actions and next steps in life. However, if we wish to tap more deeply into our mission in life or, alternatively, to choose more properly in crucial junctions in our life, it is recommended to do it with an authorized White Light instructor. The reason for this is twofold: the techniques used by the instructors are far more complex and thorough, and the ability of an experienced person to assist us in watching our life from a bird's eye view is an invaluable gift.

Practice: The Expansion of a Question

1. Close your eyes and relax deeply. Breathe slowly and deeply, and relax more and more with every breath you take... In this relaxed and open state, examine: if you could ask only one question, what question would you like to ask the unknown, God or life? ...

2. Now, try, as much as possible, to move into the sacred space of the question in a light, airy and transparent spirit. In order to enter the sacred space, you need to become as open as the sky... as vast as the ocean... as still as

a lake... and as innocent as a child... To enable this, examine if there is any unnecessary and excessive baggage that you carry in regard to the issue of the question (... the question from section 1) and that might weigh you down and prevent you from being light, airy and transparent: sensations, emotions, thoughts, presumptions... Before you enter, put aside all this different, burdensome baggage... You can always return to it at the end of the process, but now, let yourself be as airy, innocent and light as possible. Let your mind be free, and move toward the question...

3. From this state of relaxation and honest intent to receive a true answer, listen to the question (... the question from section 1). Hold the question while breathing into it and letting go even more. Feel the question...Try to describe it in words. What does it feel like? ... Look for an area in the body... a shape or an image... a color... a general sensation... a fragrance...

4. Breathe into the mystery of the question (... the question from section 1). Feel it from within. Remember: the question is like a transparent gate through which you are about to move into the unknown... Let it spread wider and deeper. Fill your entire body and being. Breathe into the (... shape or image) and into the (... area of the body), and let it expand more and more, until it reaches its outermost limit, until it cannot expand anymore. Request: "question, show yourself completely to me!" ...

5. You have now entered the space of the question. Examine what you see, sense, feel and know... Even if at first there is only deep stillness, move deeply into this relaxation and then look around you: What do you see in regard to the question (... the question from section 1)? ... Examine whether the question has changed or remained as it was before. If it is a new question, let the new question form within your depths...

6. Leave behind whatever you have seen so far and continue on your journey. Now, focus your entire attention and listen to the question: (... the question from section 5) ... Stay with the question; be present, with a brain devoid of reaction, judgment or movement. Get in touch with the question. Move into its very heart, into its core. Try to describe it in words. What does it feel like? ... Look for an area in the body... a shape or an image... a color... a general sensation... a fragrance...

7. Breathe into the mystery of the question (... the question from section 5). Feel it from within. Let it spread wider and deeper. Fill your entire body and being. Breathe into the (... shape or image) and into the (... area of the body), and let it expand more and more, until it reaches its outermost limit, until it cannot expand anymore. Request: "question, show yourself completely to me!" ...

8. You have now entered the space of the question. Examine what you see, sense, feel and know... Even if at first there is only deep stillness, move deeply into this relaxation and then look around you: What do you see in regard to the question (... the question from section 5)? ... Examine whether the question has changed or remained as it was before. If it is a new question, let the new question form within your depths...

9. Leave behind whatever you have seen so far and continue on your journey. Now, focus your entire attention and listen to the question: (... the question from section 8) ... Give yourself up and let the question fill your mind and body. Don't look for an answer; rather, discover the beauty and ecstasy of the very presence of the question, the tremendous expanses of opportunities that it allows, and the magic of not knowing. Get in touch with the question. Move into its very heart, into its core. Try to describe it in words. What does it feel like? ... Look for

an area in the body... a shape or an image... a color... a general sensation... a fragrance...

10. Breathe into the mystery of the question (... the question from section 8). Feel it from within. Let it spread wider and deeper. Fill your entire body and being. Breathe into the (... shape or image) and into the (... area of the body), and let it expand more and more, until it reaches its outermost limit, until it cannot expand anymore. Request: "question, show yourself completely to me!" ...

11. You have now entered the space of the question. Examine what you see, sense, feel and know... Even if at first there is only deep stillness, move deeply into this relaxation and then look around you: What do you see in regard to the question (... the question from section 8)? ... Look for an area in the body... a shape or an image... a color... a general sensation... a fragrance...

12. For the last time, breathe into the mystery of the question (... the question from section 8). Feel it from within. Let it spread wider and deeper. Fill your entire body and being. Breathe into the (... shape or image) and into the (... area of the body), and let it expand more and more, until it reaches its outermost limit, until it cannot expand anymore. Request: "question, show yourself completely to me!" ...

13. Give a name to this expanded state... You have now reached a space in which everything seems to be already resolved and no question has ever existed... From this state, wash your brain with White Light... Wash any confusion or doubt that existed in you at the beginning of the process, when you first raised the question...

14. Feel, in this space, the awakened presence of your inner teacher. Feel the intelligence, the wisdom, the all-inclusive seeing... Now let the inner teacher listen to the question: (... the question from section 8) - what can the inner teacher tell you about this question? ... Look for

instructions and practical guidance... Continue to guide yourself until the answer seems clear enough... How would you act and respond in your life in light of this new clarity? ...

15. Remember that this expanded state is not only the source of your clarity and wisdom but also your true home. Before you open your eyes, you can choose to stay in contact with this state within your heart even in your ordinary state of consciousness... For the last time, immerse yourself in the state... Now, you can slowly and gently open your eyes.

A Sharing

I., 35 years old, after an experience of the "Expansion of a Question," which he defines as "an event that has changed my life."

I entered this process with the question, 'How should I behave in the present conflict with my parents?' This conflict centered on my confrontations with their constant criticism about my life. I came confused and fearful, and I had to unload a lot of emotional baggage: the fear of doing something too extreme, the fear of losing their financial support and even the fear of finding out that they were actually right in their criticism. At the beginning of the process I felt a horrible constriction in my throat and tension in my jaw and chest. I was inflamed with internal violence

Eventually, I defined the precise question: 'What is the ideal way to manage the relationship between me and my parents?' Then, I started expanding. It was like a journey along which even angers from my early childhood surfaced, while, at the same time, expanses of freedom and knowing, which made it possible to leave behind the mental prison, were revealed. The question crumbled, as it were, my psychological structure and gave way to love and compassion. I could see their hearts and remember that at their core they were "souls" on their own journey and that they too wished for the good while lacking the knowledge to fully realize this goodness.

Listening to the question quieted my brain more and more. I felt as if my ability to see were "stretched out" over 360 degrees, and there was a new flow of intelligence. At once, I realized that the solution had to spring from a wide-open vision; that I had to share this sight with my parents as a gift, instead of throwing aggressive criticism at them that leads nowhere.

Unbelievably, along the expansions, the horrifying question turned into infinite ecstasy, a glowing White Light; it was as if I were stepping into mystery and grace! I experienced it as if a wise teacher woke up in me, a teacher that could illuminate the path for my hurting and paining present self. I could see that I was the adult in charge of this matter, and that I shouldn't expect anything from them since they were incapable of seeing it themselves at the present stage. I'm completely alone, and this is my lesson: to learn to take on the responsibility for myself and to become my own parent. Whatever I expected them to be, I should become myself: a source of abundance, grace, beauty and light.

I must tell them the truth, in clear and penetrating words, without expecting anything and without having my happiness and wholeness dependent on their affirmation and acceptance. I must express the truth simply and peacefully, devoid of emotion and free from the sense of being the victim, and whatever they may choose to do with it is not "my business." Simply put, I should speak out everything, fearlessly, in order to release the suffocation in the throat; I should stop keeping quiet and accumulating tension within. Even if they get a little hurt, this might contribute, in the long run, to the solidity of our relationship. I must always leave the door open to them, yet learn how to be natural with them.

In general, I saw that I should live my life independent from them, financially too, and if they would wish to join such a life, as part of a flow of love, so much the better. They, too, go through a maturation process as parents, and their way of coping with my truth allows them to work on themselves. I have reached a stage in which I'm allowed to expect a relationship based on basic mutual respect—such a relationship has never taken place between us so far. I'm not their little boy anymore!

These insights have liberated me extraordinarily and, shortly after, opened the door to a new level of relationship between us.

Shai Tubali

11

The Dirt Track and the Freeway

So far, we have deeply examined the great potential revealed through the Theory of Subtle Fields and the expansion process, both on the psychological-therapeutic plane and on the plane of creativity and practical life. Now, we will find out about the implications of the White Light method on the way in which we understand and realize the spiritual dimension of life.

Before anything else, the very concept of "spirituality" radically transforms. Spirituality, in the present context, will be *the conscious process of the expansion of consciousness*—the process of awakening the five fields, as well as progressively settling in them. From this follows a highly important understanding: genuine spiritual development is only the shift from one level of consciousness to another, higher or more expanded, level of consciousness. In this way, the spiritual "destination," which tends, too often, to be obscured, becomes dramatically clear.

When we laid out the five fundamentals of the expansion process at the beginning of the book, a certain distinction was made, one that we should return to now, this time in the spiritual context: the distinction between the "dirt track" and the "freeway."

The popular "dirt track" is the spiritual journey that takes place on the planes of the brain and the mental-emotional field: a persistent and arduous journey from point X to point Y, while point X is our state as it is and Y is our sought-after future state. Y is the total opposite of X; it is the self-change promised to us if we only pace toward it with resolve and all our might.

For instance, if we are angry people, the spiritual journey will appeal to us as a way to reduce anger and increase patience and forgiveness in our life; if we are fear-ridden, we will be attracted toward meditation in the hope of reducing anxieties and establishing trust in life and others, and if we are subjected to a relentless attack of thoughts and emotions, a longing to be less and less in the "head" and more and more "here and now" will arise within us.

From these examples, we can clearly see how the spiritual destination is always the complementary opposite of the present state. In fact, to a great extent, the spiritual destination is a concept, an idea or an ideal that is viewed, within our mind, as being against the negative and troublesome state of affairs. Accordingly, one can look at the development of any spiritual concept throughout history. For example, because of our intense inclination to attach to and cling to people and things, the doctrine of non-attachment gradually evolved in the "dirt track," and because of the narcissistic and selfish nature of our current level of thought, many known practices for the cultivation of compassion and love have emerged from the "dirt track." All meditation practices of the "dirt track" are nothing but reactions, complementary contrasts to "what is," to the present reality of our being and life: if you are tense—learn to breathe and let go; if you are too identified with your emotions—learn to observe; if you do not notice anything except for your thoughts—turn your attention to the present and appreciate what you already have.

The "dirt track" is, therefore, a conceptual spirituality: all of its ideas stem from complementary opposites, which is our life as it is. Those who tread on this path inevitably cling to these notions, which bestow on them consolation and the sense of getting closer to a target (which is, of course, attainting a state of "happiness," the complementary opposite of the state of suffering). "Accept your life as it is;" "Everything is the will of the universe (or God or life);" "Be here and now"—these are only examples of the various thought-forms that the brain espouses for the sake of achieving longed for psycho-spiritual health.

For thousands of years, humanity has tread on the "dirt track"—the path of suffering and hope, fear and belief, lack of change and conceptual spirituality. All along the way it has held on to the hope for increasing improvement, yet the human brain, in its psychological foundations, has only transformed through it a little. The reason for this is obvious: a genuine evolution of the brain cannot take place through the current level of consciousness but only by leaping to a new level of consciousness.

The expansion process along the fields reveals to us, through direct experience, not only that the gradual shift from X to Y fails to work but also that it is totally unnecessary. After all, the expansion, which leads us *directly* to the subtle fields, releases us, in doing so, from the present level of consciousness, which is completely made of opposites, contrasts and contradictions. An expansion leads us to total freedom from the X, and thus also makes the Y completely irrelevant.

Already in the shift to the third, mental-spiritual field, this freedom is achieved. This freedom is not the outcome of the struggle to shift from a state of non-freedom to freedom, but rather the opposite-free nature of the new, broader level of consciousness. As we reside in this level of consciousness, we can no longer comprehend the need for conceptual spirituality: Why should we cultivate "non-attachment" when we are complete and totally independent anyway? And why is it so important to strive to become a "good" and "loving" person, when, in the third field, "goodness" and "love" are an effortless outflow of the completeness and harmony of our being? And who needs to be "here and now" when dwelling in the field is being beyond time?

Through the expansion process we directly realize what "transformative spirituality" means; transformations as actual modifications of form and as a passage from one level of consciousness to an entirely new level of consciousness, in which all contexts, ways of interpretation and fundamental concepts change beyond recognition. Transformative spirituality is revealed, then, as a journey that is clearly distinguished from the journey of gradual change, which characterizes the "dirt track."

Without a doubt, the very fact that we instill awareness, alertness and intention into our lives—through the "dirt track"—makes our processes of change far more intense and accelerated, unlike the majority of people, who tend to change only against their will and under the tremendous pressures of external life. However, only the "freeway" can provide us with the keys for true development, which implies leaping to a level of consciousness that completely exceeds the stifling limitations of the familiar human experience.

Whereas the "dirt track" cultivates concepts, beliefs, customs, rituals and the repetition of some emotion or another, the "freeway" focuses on *settling in more expanded levels of consciousness*. Despite the name given to it, its great value does not lie merely in being "faster" (although it is definitely faster!) but even more so, in being far more direct: instead of toiling over the improvement of the present level of consciousness, which is, by nature, conflicted and laden with inner contradictions, it guides our consciousness in a way that is simultaneously moving vertically and expanding toward incredibly evolved planes of consciousness.

On the "freeway" the ability to awaken the subtle fields and to move within them is rapidly enhanced, yet there is no skipping of any of the stages; in order to truly separate from the present level of consciousness, man must carry out a simultaneous process of unraveling memory connections in the mental-emotional field and deepening into the fields of consciousness. These concurrent processes are vital since as long as the brain itself is not free from psychological memory, we will have to return, at the end of any memory-releasing technique, to the conditioned level of consciousness. Anyway, these two aspects of the developmental process are completely available through the White Light method.

That being said, there is no need to untie *all* memory connections in the mental-emotional field in order to step beyond its boundaries. Every person has a number of major memory connections that shape his limited personality and, as such, constitute the prime obstacles to the evolution of his consciousness. These obstacles must be thoroughly lifted through "positive therapy," while the person continues to drink his fill of true bliss and inspiration from incessant experiences of total freedom, which are accessible to him at any given moment with expansion. The act of expansion habituates him to disconnecting, again and again, from the whole gamut of thoughts, emotions, desires and fears of the familiar level of consciousness, as well as residing, longer and longer, in the subtle fields.

The "freeway" is not a path that is waiting for some sort of divine grace that might redeem us from our miseries. It is the other way around: this is a path that is characterized by the fundamental understanding of absolute self-responsibility and substantial self-effort. The "dirt track" is a road of hope and anticipation, but the "freeway" is a path of evolution that we are able to fulfill with our own two hands. It is in our power to develop our consciousness—the more we devote energy and awareness to such a process, the more we may earn the fruits of our labor. No grace is involved in the process of untying memory connections, and no grace is involved in our ability to penetrate the fields of consciousness and to abide in them to our heart's content. Every technique in the White Light is living proof that readiness and self-effort are enough to attain extraordinarily expanded states of consciousness. Does this not imply that the grace is us?

For many ages, esoteric seers have pointed out the existence of fields (or hidden bodies), but this has usually served more as a mapping of consciousness than as a practical tool that can be activated by the power of intention. By activating them now through our awareness and free will, a gateway has opened for us to discover ourselves as a consciousness that is essentially not psychological, as a spiritual consciousness. From that follows that, in many respects, we are already free from the psychological thicket, and we are not obliged to identifying ourselves with it—and therefore, we no longer have any excuse for suffering.

Some may claim that it is still better to combine the "freeway" and the "dirt track," feeling that the "dirt track" is more humane and patient with the slow and gradual processes we require for change. However, such a claim mostly stems from a lack of deep acquaintance with the "freeway" in which, undoubtedly, there is a gradual process—after all, this is not a narrow and flat road, and, on each and every plane along its way, one must undergo an all-inclusive and meticulous alignment of the entire being, from thought to emotion to the last cell in the body.

What often hides behind the reluctance to forgo the "dirt track" is the fact that this path endows us with a feeling of relief—whereas the "freeway" evokes in us some sort of tension and unease that stems from the feeling of evolutionary pressure. For those whose basic experience of life is sufficiently positive, an evolutionary pressure should not cause too great a resistance, but for people who possess a fundamentally negative experience of life, this pressure will be felt as a rather unfair demand to rise above their present condition. As long as our experience of life is negative, we will yearn for the relaxation of the "dirt track," for its comforting concepts and for its practices that strike a chord of nostalgic longing for a time, imaginary or real, in which "everything was simpler." It seems that, in this context, the most important thing is to realize that the true role of genuine spirituality is not to alleviate suffering but rather to help us evolve, maturely and responsibly, toward planes on which suffering cannot possibly exist.

Spiritual Practices on the "Dirt Track" and on the "Freeway"

A considerable number of practices aim at quieting and relaxing the brain and the mental-emotional field, as well as balancing the electromagnetic field of man. These practices, though not transformative, and usually also unpretending, have their own significance and role. Beyond this type of relaxation, many schools and traditions offer a whole range of spiritual practices (including meditation practices) that aim at a more radical transformation of man. These practices, with no exception, are different means developed for the sake of the expansion of consciousness, and in this sense, any spiritual technique directs a person, consciously or unconsciously, toward entering the subtle fields. Therefore, the White Light method is, simply, a highly conscious fulfillment of the intention that stands behind every spiritual practice in this world.

In the end, *meditation resides in the subtle fields*, and for this reason, the most efficient meditation will be the one that is capable of leading a person directly and systematically to the hidden fields of consciousness (correspondingly, an inefficient meditation will be the one that leads us to a state of relaxation in which we remain entrapped in the our present level of consciousness). According to this definition, many White Light techniques are suitable to serve as "substitutes" for the traditional meditation practices.

In general, there are three types of relaxation, calming down—or, put more accurately, "silence:"

1. The silence of emptying oneself from thoughts.

2. The silence of going beyond thoughts.

3. The all-encompassing silence.

The silence of emptying oneself from thoughts, which characterizes the practices of the "dirt track," is random and unintentional quietude that is brought about as a result of the energy accumulated within us during meditation or any spiritual practice. In the terminology of the expansion process, this silence has an "end" and a "limit," and yet it is greatly significant when it comes to the balance of body and mind. In certain moments we find ourselves moving or *sinking* into a state of extremely deep relaxation, and everything "comes to a halt" within us. Whenever such a temporary state is achieved, we gain highly positive internal nourishment.

In contrast to that, the silence of going beyond thoughts (which characterizes many of the known practices of the "freeway" and is connected with the mental-spiritual field) allows us to transcend to a broader plane of consciousness, in which familiar thought cannot exist. This is, then, a state beyond the mental plane, an ecstatic plain that precedes the world of thought. In this free state, a great deal of energy awakens within us, as if we come across a ceaseless spring of energy that fills the entire fabric of body and mind. In this type of silence, a substantial release is made possible since we cease to depend on circumstances and changes and are able to discover emotions that we have always hoped to find in the world outside us within ourselves. We find our true liberty with the discovery that, through this silence, we can bestow on ourselves an unconditioned happiness and a non-causal satisfaction. The third, rarer type of silence is the all-encompassing silence (associated with the fifth field of pure awareness). This silence is not a new or higher level—this is the silence in which all levels of consciousness exist; everything is included within it since it is the expanse or the open space in which every condition and every thing, the entire universe actually, appears. It is beyond freedom and non-freedom, and therefore it does not depend on states, even the most remarkable states of transcendence. The American philosopher Ken Wilber explains it through the following beautiful metaphor: if we imagine that all levels of consciousness are written, one by one, on a paper, this type of silence is the paper itself, the page on which all levels appear.

It is in the power of the expansion process of the White Light to lead the person, over and over again in the most systematic way, to the non-causal state of the silence beyond thoughts—and, in some of the practices of the method, it is also possible to achieve, over and over again, the all-encompassing silence. The latter is quite unique since the all-encompassing silence is very difficult, even impossible to reach via a technique—after all, this state is usually considered, by its very nature, "unattainable!"

White Light meditation

Basically, any White Light practice may be considered a daily meditation, and any object we may choose to expand, from a negative emotion to a philosophical idea, can serve us in this meditation. With the distinctive use of the expansion process for the sake of meditation—as opposed to its more practical uses for the purpose of therapy or creative action –the expansion itself and prolonged immersion in the subtle fields become a purpose unto themselves. Thus, as soon we attain an expanded state of consciousness, we may abide in it to our heart's content, and in this way, contact our true self intensely, the one that exists beyond thought and the upheavals of life.

In like manner, you can enhance your current meditation practices, whatever they may be, through the process of expansion. This might require you to exercise a certain degree of daring, as this implies deviating from the traditional approach in regard to this practice. But if you find the boldness to try out, it is very likely that you will discover your meditation becomes immeasurably more effective. Practitioners of "Zazen"—the Zen-Buddhist practice of still meditation—can perform, from time to time along the practice, an expansion of the pure presence or the sense of "here and now;" practitioners of Vipassana—the Buddhist practice of observation—can perform expansions of significant sensations that are revealed in the body, and practitioners of Transcendental Meditation can perform an expansion of their mantra every few minutes. Keep in mind the purpose of the expansion process: the realization of the highest or most expanded potential of each and every thing, the potential of your spiritual practice included.

For someone who is not a practitioner of any sort of traditional meditation, or for anyone interested in experimenting with something new, a very simple technique for a daily practice is presented here. In the "White Light for Essences and Ideas" you can carry out the process of expansion in relation to one of the fundamental elements or forces of life and the universe: truth, love, freedom, God, death, grace, and so on. You can also use this form for mantras or spiritual symbols. In this way you may get in much more direct touch with the essential truth beyond these common concepts. From one expansion to another you will be able to dive deeper into the third, mental-spiritual field, and thus realize within you the most profound secret of this essence.

Practice: The Expansion of Essences and Ideas

1. Close your eyes. Breathe slowly and deeply. Relax more and more with every breath you take… Choose the essence idea you would like to explore and unveil… Hold it within your mind for the next few minutes. Let it reveal itself in its fullest, most powerful presence inside your mind. Focus your attention on its core, on the mystery that surrounds it and also lies hidden right at its center. Let this essence reflect back to you your personal feelings and thoughts… What comes up inside of you in regard to the idea? …

2. Now you are about to enter into the mystery of this idea. Feel the idea deeply. Move into its core, into its very heart. Try to describe it in words. What does it feel like? … Look for an area in the body that is deeply connected to it… a shape or an image… a color… a sensation… a fragrance…

3. Feel this idea from within. Breathe into it. Allow it to spread wider and deeper. Let it fill your entire body and being. Breathe into the image or shape in the area of the body you have located, and let it expand more and more, until it reaches its outermost limit, until it cannot expand anymore. Request: "idea, show yourself completely to me!" …

4. Give a name to the expanded idea… Breathe into the expanded idea. Move into its depth, into its very core. Try to describe it in words. What does it feel like? … How do you relate to the idea from this expanded state? … Now look for an area in the body that is deeply connected to this state… a shape or an image… a color… a general sensation… a fragrance…

5. Feel the expanded idea from within. Breathe into it. Allow it to spread wider and deeper. Let it fill your entire body and being. Breathe into the image or shape in the area of the body you have located, and let it expand more and more, until it reaches its outermost limit, until it cannot expand anymore. Request: "expanded idea, show yourself completely to me!" …

6. Give a name to the expanded state… Breathe into the expanded state. Move into its depth, into its very core. Try to describe it in words. What does it feel like? … How do you relate to the idea from this expanded state? … Now look for an area in the body that

is deeply connected to this state... a shape or an image... a color... a general sensation... a fragrance...

5. Feel the expanded state from within. Breathe into it. Allow it to spread wider and deeper. Let it fill your entire body and being. Breathe into the image or shape in the area of the body you have located, and let it expand more and more, until it reaches its outermost limit, until it cannot expand anymore. Request: "expanded state, show yourself completely to me!" ...

6. Give a name to the expanded state... Breathe into the expanded state. Move into its depth, into its very core. Try to describe it in words. What does it feel like? ... How do you relate to the idea from this expanded state? ... Now look for an area in the body that is deeply connected to this state... a shape or an image... a color... a general sensation... and a fragrance...

5. Feel the expanded state from within. Breathe into it. Allow it to spread wider and deeper. Let it fill your entire body and being. Breathe into the image or shape in the area of the body you have located, and let it expand more and more, until it reaches its outermost limit, until it cannot expand anymore. Request: "expanded state, show yourself completely to me!" ...

6. Give a name to the expanded state... Breathe into the expanded state. Move into its depth, into its very core. Try to describe it in words. What does it feel like? ... How do you relate to the idea from this expanded state? ...

7. You have reached the secret of the essential idea. From this secret, wash your entire being with White Light. Wash it with a healing and liberating White Light that changes it to the core by steeping your being in illuminated reality. Ask your body and mind: "Transform yourself into the light of the essential idea!" ...

8. Now can you see what hides within the essential idea? ... Examine: who are you in this state? ... From this state, merge into the essential idea in its entirety, until you feel there is no difference, distance or barrier between you and this principle... How do you perceive your life from this state of unity with the essential idea? ... Draw on this powerful cosmic force that can empower your life as a whole...

9. For the last time, immerse yourself in this expanded state for self-remembrance and liberation... Before you open your eyes, within your heart, choose to keep in contact with this state even in your ordinary state of consciousness... Now you may gently open your eyes...

12

Spiritual Enlightenment and the Subtle Fields

Enlightenment is the elusive and abstract state of consciousness reported by the spiritual teachers of all traditions along the last thousands of years. Whether it is the "Nirvana" and "Sunyata" of Gautama the Buddha, the "Atman" and "Brahman" of Yoga, the "Ein Sof" (infinity) and "Ain" (nothingness) of Kabala or any other unique term derived from the world of spiritual cultures, it is but a different depiction of one and only one state. The more we delve into the process of expansion, and increasingly shatter through the known limits of our consciousness, the more this state becomes our direct and persistent experience, and far more than that—a far-reaching evolutionary possibility awaiting us beyond any limit or edge.

Naturally, at the earlier stages of our practice, we will still experience, over and over again, our "ceiling of experience." For instance, we will reach the enchanting expanses of the third, mental-spiritual field, and even this will seem to us unbounded and infinite. Yet, from time to time, what we tended to consider limitless, would be revealed as a structure that is expandable, and our consciousness would begin to contact the real infinity that lies totally beyond the boundaries of perception and knowing.

We can liken this to landing in a new and exotic country. The moment we start walking on the streets, we might undergo a "culture shock" and wander on them, helplessly lost. We will not comprehend the language, and the customs of the place will appear extremely odd to us. Yet, if we repeatedly land at that country, we will slowly but surely adjust to it and, eventually, even delight in it; we will be able to navigate our way and properly communicate with the inhabitants of the place. This image totally befits the first encounters with the mental-spiritual field: like a new country, our consciousness must adapt to the new and unknown expanses, and only when it has a good command of them, will it be able to confidently feel its way toward the fourth, cosmic-soul field, and later on, toward the fifth, pure awareness field.

In the first chapters of this book, we related the process of the "contraction" of the divine light that enabled the formation and crystallization of different structures. We demonstrated how everything in the universe—a thought, an elephant or a human personality—is a structure with its own defined characteristics and boundaries and explained that expansion is actually the reverse process: shattering the limits of the structure so it "returns," as it were, to the primal, totally expanded state, in which there were no characteristics and boundaries. This state is the primordial being prior to creation (or, in our terminology, prior to any "contraction").

The process of expansion, as it is applied in the White Light method, is precisely striving toward the primordial being. Since in every structure in the universe there lies the ancient memory of the state that preceded all contractions, all structures have an innate longing to "go back" to the unbounded being through absolute release of limitations. Limits and contractions—conscious or unconscious—are the most primal suffering of each and every structure, whereas expansion, the return to the primordial state, is the most profound happiness available to us. Whenever we experience a loss of limitations and feel ourselves vast, "beyond ourselves," we are filled with supreme bliss. The conscious longing for a vast state is the very urge that pulls us into the spiritual journey.

One need not go as far as the fifth field to recognize the reality of this principle in our personal life too. If we deeply examine our recollections of happiness, it will become clear to us that our most powerful moments of happiness were characterized by the sense of the shattering of limitation, expansion and going out of and beyond the limits of ourselves. Many people seek such experiences of utter self-forgetfulness through psychedelic drugs, alcohol, limit-experiences, sex and even power-intoxication. In stark contrast to that, negative experiences are always associated with the sense of limitation, as if everything became narrow, impossible and stifling.

Enlightenment is, simply put, transcendence beyond any sense of limitation, the expanding of consciousness "to infinity and beyond." In the language of the White Light, the state of Enlightenment is revealed and fulfilled on the broadest edges of the fifth field, on the borderline interfacing with the fifth field of the universe itself.

The fifth field, in its increasing realization, is the field through which we get in touch and unite our consciousness with the pure and primordial being. In its light, even the third and fourth fields are revealed as structures—as confined structures with limits and sidewalls, characteristics and attributes. The fifth field is the only one that can connect our consciousness to "that" which is not a structure, that which is the source of all structures, that—which may be called "God." Hence, when the fifth field is realized, our "ceiling of experience" completely shatters and we find ourselves in a state of being that can no longer be considered an experience.

On the way to shattering the "ceiling of experience" we will, more and more, become acquainted with the subtle layers of the universal unity—a unity that our current physics points to in every possible way and that can be known as a direct experience only through the hidden fields. Along the entire way we will have to face the cultural conditioning, which stems primarily from monotheistic religions, that "God" is a something or a someone, due to the fact that our direct experience will lead us to the complete opposite—to states of being which are devoid of characteristics and attributes, empty of substantial content, formless and free of any sentimental emotion. Thus it will become more and more clear to us that the real "God" is precisely that utter emptiness, just as Gautama the Buddha pointed out so well about 2600 years ago, and in this sense, he is completely different from the "God of thought," the image of God created by the very hands of human thought. Such a revelation is particularly earth-shattering for religious people. Nevertheless, its authenticity is undeniable: at last, for the first time, the brain contacts something that is totally beyond it, something that it cannot invent by itself and also cannot control, and its thoughts are unable to achieve it or put it in a tiny memory box.

If we wish to fully succeed in such a journey, we must be prepared not to stop at any station along the way, as comfortable and thrilling as it may be. More than others, the third, mental-spiritual field endows us with a whole world of exciting experiences: the cessation of suffering and the emergence of emotions of deep contentment and love; mystical symbols and visions; powerful intuitions and the awakening of occult vision, and states of profound silence and being in the "here and now," beyond time. In this field, we experience, for the first time, true freedom from all psychological and even physical dependency, and for this reason, many are tempted to stop here and to be content with it as the "ceiling of experience." Often, people also tend to confuse it with the "Bodhi state" of the fifth field. That is why we should insist, all along the way, on exceeding any limit and any kind of structure, even the subtlest, most spiritual structures, in order to realize Enlightenment—the only state that is completely liberated from all structures.

The Great Union

The theory of fields enables us to explain the mystery of the enlightened state more deeply. As we repeatedly practice the process of expansion, we succeed in awakening our five fields of consciousness and even strengthening our relation to them more and more. With the passing of time, through a concentrated self-effort, we may even become established in the subtle fields, which means that we will get used to identifying ourselves with them even in our daily state of consciousness. The more this process deepens, the more a wondrous thing begins to take place: through our individual five fields we contact the five fields of the universe.

Along with our spiritual maturation, a progressive alignment begins to occur between the individual five fields and the five fields of the universe. It is no longer a random connection between them. A random connection may be enabled through different spiritual experiences, and sometimes even through psychedelic drugs and psychoactive plants; for instance, contact with the spiritual dimensions of the universe that reside in its mental-spiritual field or contact with "cosmic meditation," the omnipresent ground of being as it is revealed in its field of pure awareness. Nevertheless, alignment between the individual fields and the universal fields is an entirely different occurrence: its aim is to bring about a mergence between the personal consciousness and the divine consciousness, an inconceivable state of oneness in which the person can no longer distinguish between "himself" and the "universe" or the "universal self." In the spirit of the Sufi tradition, one can liken it to a relationship between a lover and a beloved. At the first stage, brief contacts of union take place, yet there is an ever-increasing longing to remove the boundaries completely and merge into one another through an act of lovemaking from which there is no return.

As the connections between the individual fields and the cosmic fields solidify, the individual undergoes a tremendous reversal of self-identity: from personal, private and separate identity, one shifts to a universal, all-embracing identity. He no longer only "experiences" an interaction with the extensive fields of the universe momentarily since his selfhood unites with the one and only self, the self of all that is. More and more, his energic senses, referred to as "fields," magnetize the cosmic fields toward them and are filled with them—until, eventually, the great union occurs: the individual fields are assimilated into the more expanded fields, and the cosmic identity turns into a permanent state.

The process of assimilating the individual fields into the general fields is gradual: at first, an intense cosmic prana flows from the electromagnetic field of the universe into man's subtle anatomy (the Chakra system and the central column, primarily via the Crown Chakra); then "divine" emotions and thoughts, such as supreme bliss and connection to infinity, flow out of the mental-emotional fields of the universe into the thoughts and feelings of man's mental-emotional field; in due time, the person is filled with the sense of divine existence beyond time and space, along with its countless dimensions and layers (third field), with the unity consciousness and divine truth (fourth field), and finally, with the absolute divine being of the fifth cosmic field. The individual fields are filled more and more with the cosmic energy, and the latter re-aligns them—and following them, the brain and the entire body undergo re-alignment as well. At a certain moment, when the energy of the fourth and fifth cosmic fields begins to stream, the unification of the fields takes place and "Enlightenment" comes into being.

As a result of the great union a "baby" is born for the lover and the beloved; a new shared field that combines the individual consciousness and the universal consciousness, a wondrous blend of man and "God."

The Expansion of Self-Identity

Throughout this entire book, we have demonstrated over and over again our remarkable ability to expand our consciousness. However, it is easy to get confused and to think that "consciousness" is something that we possess, some sort of an object that we expand again and again. If we wish to attain Enlightenment, we must remind ourselves that, in the deepest sense, *consciousness is who we are*—in fact, it is *our* broadest self, and hence the expansion process enables us to become acquainted with subtler planes and layers of our very own self. It is very likely that we become aware of that when we toil over the unraveling memory connections in the mental-emotional field, but do we understand that when our consciousness expands to infinity, this infinity is actually us?

Our true self is not concealed within us, fully developed and only waiting to be revealed, as many tend to claim. Rather, it lies within us as a dormant and highly potent seed that, if properly cultivated, will rise and grow "outwardly," toward our individual subtle fields, and from there, toward the primordial being that came prior to all creation. Just as it is thrilling to observe a tiny acorn while contemplating the fact that the potential of a whole majestic oak tree already exists within it, so too our most expanded self hides as an inconceivable possibility within our present, minuscule "I."

Unlike the common approaches of some traditions of the spirit, the "White Light method" does not seek to nullify or annihilate the sense of "I" (which is also referred to, in a spiritual and not a psychological context, as the "ego"). This is for two reasons: the first is that, in the White Light, we do not nullify anything and do not reject anything since all that "is" is a potential for an ever increasing expansion of consciousness, and the second is that a rather great destiny is reserved for our sense of "I"—in its ultimate expansion, it is revealed as no less than the divine "I" itself! In cosmological terms, the cosmos toiled for many billions of years until it managed to bring forth an organism that possessed the capacity for self-awareness, a sense of existence that knew itself—or, in other words, a conscious "I." A supreme purpose hides behind its efforts: to use this "I" as its own awareness.

We, each and every one of us, are destined to become the self-awareness of the universe itself, and for this reason, our "I" carries within it, as a seed, the capacity to grow into an all-embracing "I," one that contains the entire universe. Indeed, in the process of expansion, this is revealed as an extremely simple reality: an expansion of the sense of "I" easily leads us to a state in which we are vast to such a great extent, that there isn't, nor can there ever be, anything outside us.

In the end, the evolution—or expansion—of the sense of self is the principal goal of any spiritual journey. Each one of us has patterns and mental structures that we would love to be relieved of, if we only knew how. Yet true spirituality, a transformative spirituality, deals with the shattering of the first structure—the structure of the

"I"—through a repeated experience of smashing limitations and exceeding the boundaries of the familiar self. Exceeding the boundaries of self is not a "big deal" in the "White Light method."

It is not the sense of "I" that needs to be nullified but rather all the unnecessary layers that envelop it and conceal it from every direction: around our present "I," the pure seed of self-awareness and countless memory connections. As a result, repetitive and compulsive grooves of thought and emotion have been spun. The personality that encompasses the sense of "I" and that sucks up its entire vitality and glory is the one that needs to come apart. That is why true spirituality "releases" the sense of "I" from the entire mental, emotional and sensual thicket, until it succeeds in leaving it naked and free. This is the first and essential stage of a spiritual journey, and many meditation techniques were developed for its attainment, such as the Koan and Zazen of Zen-Buddhism, Vipassana of Buddhism and other approaches for the observation of thought, emotion and sensation.

As soon as the sense of "I" begins to be released from all the characteristics of memory that have encompassed it—circumstances, past experiences, self-definitions of all kinds and more—it continues expanding, starting on its exciting journey toward its final destination:

1. In the first expansion, in the electromagnetic field, we experience: "*I am not the body* but rather the life force that animates the body and encompasses it; I am energy, a vibration of life." Anyone who has experienced watching a man die was most likely astounded by the moment in which the life force was taken away from the body and only a lifeless corpse remained. Whatever had activated this corpse and had imbued it with personality, thought and the warmness of emotion disappeared as if it had never been. Such an example may awaken within us the sense that we are not that corpse but rather the energy that instilled life into it.

2. In the second expansion, in the mental-emotional field, we recognize the "I" that is devoid of any thought and

emotion and that exists as plain awareness or pure presence, here and now. This "I" is easily revealed, through practices of observation of thought and emotion, as a presence that is watching from afar and lacking in attributes. Here the experience is: "I am not my thoughts and emotions but rather the observer of all thoughts and emotions."

3. In the third expansion, in the mental-spiritual field, we identify ourselves thus: "I am an immortal spiritual being that exists beyond time and space; I was never born and will never die; I have always been free and will always be free, as I am undamageable and incorruptible." As previously mentioned, this is the "ceiling of experience" for many, and the tendency of many is to think that this is the liberated state of the "Buddha." Yet this is just another stage of the expansion of the "I."

4. In the fourth expansion, in the cosmic-soul field, the sense of "I" is revealed as the "I" of the whole universe, and accordingly, we identify our self as the omnipresent "I." Yet another, even deeper layer of self-identity in the cosmic-soul field is a sense of unity with the energy and intelligence that gave rise to the universe.

5. In the fifth expansion, in the pure awareness field, we identity our self in the spirit of the well-known Yogic proclamation: "I am That!" That is, I am the primordial divine self that came prior to all creation; the broadest "I" from which any sense of "I" in this universe has germinated. Here, too, a more profound layer exists, a layer of complete absorption in the primordial "no-thing"— an indescribable state.

This is but a partial depiction of the expansion process of self-identity (those interested in more than that can turn to Yogic scriptures, such as "Yoga Vasishta," or study the hierarchies delineated by great spiritual teachers such as Maharishi Mahesh Yogi), and yet it is enough to clarify this crucial point: we ought to move from the most personal to the most impersonal, from the individual to the universal, and in doing so, we need to progressively realize the latent potential of the minuscule sense of "I" with which we started our journey. Of course, the implications of such an expansion are beyond description—after all, it holds within it the thrilling understanding that, at least to some extent, God is also us.

The following technique was designed to lead you, step by step, along the process of the expansion of the "I," and thus directly connect your consciousness to the illuminated state of being. Unlike other techniques, in which we expand some object or another, here we perform an expansion of the subject itself, an expansion of our self—and for this reason precisely we are able to reach the furthest possible state of expansion: the depths of the fifth field, the field of pure awareness.

Obviously, our starting point in the technique is the basic sense of "I" that we all share. We are not used to getting into direct contact with the "I"—our contact with it is mostly made indirectly, through the countless sensations, emotions, thoughts and actions related to it. This "I" is like the roots of a thick tree. In fact, without it, one cannot sense, feel or know anything. Every person says, very simply and easily, "I think... I feel... I know... I hope... I love..." but how many of us have noticed that, at the root of all these actions, emotions and thoughts, lies, before anything else, the same, one and only, "I"? We may have come across this through meditation, when thoughts, emotions and sensations left for a moment and only a pure sense of existence remained. Therefore, we start with our fundamental sense of presence, and then pass it through five successive expansions.

The sense of "I" is the fastest and most direct path that leads to the fifth field. As soon as it is released from the circumstances of life and from the daily identities and definitions that have been attached to it, it breaks through its boundaries and, shortly after, becomes all-encompassing and infinite. But this is not enough: with every expansion we ensure that we have deeply explored the implications of the evolution of the "I," since *everything* changes as a result of the expansion of the existential sense—that is, after all, the meaning of Enlightenment. Thus, we will scan the changes in the internal qualities, the relation to the body, the worldview, the understanding of the meaning of life and our part in it, the relation to thoughts and emotions, our will, our urges and our choices in life.

This meticulous scanning of the implications of this transformation holds a tremendous significance: it is one thing to abide in an inconceivable meditative state in which we come to realize that our consciousness is, indeed, infinity itself, and it is a totally different thing to succeed in *living* in this state moment to moment. Therefore, the act of scanning at each and every stage of consciousness strives to integrate our daily and ordinary consciousness—teaching us, more and more, how to connect the broadest self to the plane of the most contracted "I" and to attain a perfect middle point between Enlightenment and life in the world. We should persistently try to learn not only how to "return" from these tremendous states into the limited body and mind but, much more than that, how to merge one with the other; how to become a divine, cosmic, illuminated and infinite presence in the visible world.

With the end of the expansion process, we will reach section 23. This section's entire purpose is to discuss the formation of deep connections between our infinite, universal self and life itself. It is likely that, after our first time performing this technique, we will find ourselves too speechless and stunned to carry out any kind of integration process. Such a difficulty is completely natural: we are not used to being that vast! A second barrier is that we might get too attached to the pure, expanded and effortless state, and we will prefer to avoid the integration, desiring distance from and even feeling abhorrence toward the misery-ridden and challenge-laden "ordinary state"—in such a case, remember that this is the expected reaction of a feeble first Chakra, an obvious temptation for a person whose experience of life is negative and who, deep inside, would rather detach from it forever. Enlightenment is not a refined and subtle means for suicide—rather, it is a re-birth within life itself. Hence, we must understand that integration is not to be considered a choice or luxury; in every sense, we

are committed to perform it, otherwise the inconceivable wonder
of our expanded being will forever remain as an unrealized seed
of inner knowing.

———————

Practice: The Expansion of Self Identity

1. Close your eyes. Breathe slowly and deeply, and relax
   more and more with every breath you take... Turn your
   focus toward your feeling of presence, your sense of self-
   existence... This is the purest sense of "I AM." This sense
   exists prior to all feelings and thoughts. It is before "I
   feel," "I think" and even before "I am alive." It is simply: "I
   am" or "I am present." Remember that what is common
   to "I live," "I understand," "I love" and "I see," is the "I" at
   the beginning of each sentence... So let go now of any
   feelings, thoughts or sensations that are usually attached
   to this sense of self-existence, and simply focus your attention, for a while, on your being itself...

2. Now, turn your awareness toward your sense of "I AM,"
   your sense of self-existence, your basic sense that "I exist"... Breathe into the "I AM." Move into its depth, into
   its very core. Try to describe it in words. What does it
   feel like? ... Look for an area in the body that is deeply
   connected to it... a shape or an image... a color... a general sensation... a fragrance...

3. Breathe into the "I AM." Feel it from within. Let it spread
   wider and deeper and fill your entire body and being.
   Breath into the (... image or shape) and into the (... area
   in the body). Breathe and expand, breathe and expand,
   until it reaches its outermost limit, until it cannot expand anymore. Request: "I AM, show yourself completely to me!" ...

4. Give a name to the expanded "I Am"... Breathe into the
   (... expanded self). Move into its depth, into its very

core. Try to describe it in words. What does it feel like? ... As the (... expanded self), what are your qualities and attributes? ... From this self, what is your relationship with the body? ... As the (... expanded self), how do you perceive the world? ... As the (... expanded self), what is your understanding of the meaning of life? ... As the (... expanded self), how do you perceive your role in the world? ... From this state, would you encounter your daily thoughts and emotions differently? ... In what way? ... What is your will as the (... expanded self)? ... From this state, would you make different choices in your life? ... What kind of choices would you make then? ... As the (... expanded self), how do you perceive the choices you've made up until now? ... Can you see how everything changes along with the change in the sense of self? ...

5. From this self, wash your entire being with White Light: emotions... thoughts... sensations... Encode the body-mind complex: "Transform yourself into the light of the (... name of expanded identity)!" ...

6. Look for an area in the body that is deeply connected to this state... a shape or an image... a color... a general sensation... a fragrance...

7. Now breathe into the (... expanded self). Feel it from within. Let it spread wider and deeper and fill your entire body and being. Breathe into the (... image or shape) and into (... the area in the body). Breathe and expand, breathe and expand, until it reaches its outermost limit, until it cannot expand anymore. Request: "(... expanded self), show yourself completely to me!" ...

8. Give a name to the expanded "I Am"... Breathe into the (... expanded self). Move into its depth, into its very core. Try to describe it in words. What does it feel like? ... As the (... expanded name), what are your qualities and attributes? ... From this self, what is your relation-

ship with the body? ... As the (... expanded self), how do you perceive the world? ... As the (... expanded self), what is your understanding of the meaning of life? ... As the (... expanded self), how do you perceive your role in the world? ... From this state, would you encounter your daily thoughts and emotions differently? ... In what way? ... What is your will as the (... expanded self)? ... From this state, would you make different choices in your life? ... What kind of choices would you make then? ... As the (... expanded self), how do you perceive the choices you've made up until now? ... Can you see how everything changes along with the change in the sense of self? ...

9. From this self, wash your entire being with White Light: emotions... thoughts... sensations... Encode the body-mind complex: "Transform yourself into the light of the (... name of expanded identity)!" ...

10. Look for an area in the body that is deeply connected to this state... a shape or an image... a color... a general sensation... a fragrance...

11. Now breathe into the (... expanded self). Feel it from within. Let it spread wider and deeper and fill your entire body and being. Breathe into the (... image or shape) and into (... the area in the body). Breathe and expand, breathe and expand, until it reaches its outermost limit, until it cannot expand anymore. Request: "(... expanded self), show yourself completely to me!" ...

12. Give a name to the expanded "I Am"... Breathe into the (... expanded self). Move into its depth, into its very core. Try to describe it in words. What does it feel like? ... As the (... expanded name), what are your qualities and attributes? ... From this self, what is your relationship with the body? ... As the (... expanded self), how do you perceive the world? ... As the (... expanded self), what is your understanding of the meaning of life? ... As the (... expanded

self), how do you perceive your role in the world? ... From this state, would you encounter your daily thoughts and emotions differently? ... In what way? ... What is your will as the (... expanded self)? ... From this state, would you make different choices in your life? ... What kind of choices would you make then? ... As the (... expanded self), how do you perceive the choices you've made up until now? ... Can you see how everything changes along with the change in the sense of self? ...

13. From this self, wash your entire being with White Light: emotions... thoughts... sensations... Encode the body-mind complex: "Transform yourself into the light of the (... name of expanded identity)!" ...

14. Look for an area in the body that is deeply connected to this state... a shape or an image... a color... a general sensation... a fragrance...

15. Now breathe into the (... expanded self). Feel it from within. Let it spread wider and deeper and fill your entire body and being. Breathe into the (... image or shape) and into (... the area in the body). Breathe and expand, breathe and expand, until it reaches its outermost limit, until it cannot expand anymore. Request: "(... expanded self), show yourself completely to me!" ...

16. Give a name to the expanded "I Am"... Breathe into the (... expanded self). Move into its depth, into its very core. Try to describe it in words. What does it feel like? ... As the (... expanded name), what are your qualities and attributes? ... From this self, what is your relationship with the body? ... As the (... expanded self), how do you perceive the world? ... As the (... expanded self), what is your understanding of the meaning of life? ... As the (... expanded self), how do you perceive your role in the world? ... From this state, would you encounter your daily thoughts and emotions differently? ... In what way? ... What is your will as the (... expand-

ed self)? ... From this state, would you make different choices in your life? ... What kind of choices would you make then? ... As the (... expanded self), how do you perceive the choices you've made up until now? ... Can you see how everything changes along with the change in the sense of self? ...

17. From this self, wash your entire being with White Light: emotions... thoughts... sensations... Encode the body-mind complex: "Transform yourself into the light of the (... name of expanded identity)!" ...

18. Look for an area in the body that is deeply connected to this state... a shape or an image... a color... a general sensation... a fragrance...

19. Now breathe into the (... expanded self). Feel it from within. Let it spread wider and deeper and fill your entire body and being. Breathe into the (... image or shape) and into (... the area in the body). Breathe and expand, breathe and expand, until it reaches its outermost limit, until it cannot expand anymore. Request: "(... expanded self), show yourself completely to me!" ...

20. Give a name to the expanded "I Am"... Breathe into the (... expanded self). Move into its depth, into its very core. Try to describe it in words. What does it feel like? ... As the (... expanded name), what are your qualities and attributes? ... From this self, what is your relationship with the body? ... As the (... expanded self), how do you perceive the world? ... As the (... expanded self), what is your understanding of the meaning of life? ... As the (... expanded self), how do you perceive your role in the world? ... From this state, would you encounter your daily thoughts and emotions differently? ... In what way? ... What is your will as the (... expanded self)? ... From this state, would you make different choices in your life? ... What kind of choices would you make then? ... As the (... expanded self), how do you perceive the choices you've made up

until now? ... Can you see how everything changes along with the change in the sense of self? ...

21. From this self, wash your entire being with White Light: emotions... thoughts... sensations... Encode the body-mind complex: "Transform yourself into the light of the (... name of expanded identity)!" ...

22. Look for an area in the body that is deeply connected to this state... a shape or an image... a color... a general sensation... a fragrance...

23. Do you realize that this is who *you are*? That this is not one more experience of one state or another but rather your innermost Self? ... You are (... name of identity from section 20)... Yes, we have returned to your primordial Self—from your most contracted self back to your most expanded identity... Tell me your story as the (... name of expanded self from section 20), your journey from genesis onward - make sure the story is in the first person... What are your goals on this journey? What are your wishes on this journey? ... Perceive yourself in your entirety, from the most expanded to the most contracted and personal... Now allow your most expanded Self to enter into the most contracted self, which is connected with a specific body and mind in time and space—allow the expanded Self, the (... expanded self from section 20), to flow into the contracted self through the (... expanded self from section 16), and from the (... expanded self from section 16) through the (... expanded self from section 12), and from the (... expanded self from section 12) through the (... expanded self from section 8), and from the (... expanded self from section 8) through the (... expanded self from section 4)—until it finally reaches the initial, most limited "I AM"... Then, look at your present life from this identity. What is your relationship with your personal life now? ... Examine closely: How does this expanded self, the (... expanded self from sec-

tion 20), live in the world of time and space? ... How would you behave and act from now on according to your expanded identity of (... expanded self from section 20)? ... Are there new impulses appearing from within, impulses that arise from your real ancient journey? ... Don't stop until you can see the entire connection and bridge between the expanded Self, the (... expanded self from section 20), and your most ordinary and limited experience in the body—Can you see the connection? ...

24. Encode the body-mind complex to this important and profound remembrance: "Body-mind complex, transform yourself into the expanded Self that I am!" ... Before you open your eyes, you can choose to remain in contact with this identity within your heart, even in your ordinary state of consciousness. For the last time, immerse yourself in the expanded identity of the (... expanded self from section 20) and deepen the self-remembrance and liberation... Now you may gently open your eyes.

Sharing

E., 62 years old, after his first experience of the "White Light for self-identity."

This was an inner journey the likes of which I had never known before! I started it by identifying the sense of "I" at the center of the body as some sort of bright, elliptic shape, but already, in the first expansion, I leaped to a state that I referred to as, *"The source of thought."* From this state, which was connected to the heart, there was an incessant, radiant gush of wisdom. The body was no longer relevant. At the most, it was only a tool for this wisdom. The meaning of life on this plane was to serve as a "conductor" of the wisdom, and to pass on knowledge to all. Everything became focused, yet, at the same time, far more flowing.

In the second expansion, I reached *"Radiant love;"* a golden ray of light that only wishes to expand and cover all that is. The state was characterized by the wish to give to others from the great abundance that I possess. The world was revealed as an arena of mutual influences in which one should harmoniously partake and become an involved part; the more open I am, so I learned, the greater my participation in the general endeavor is.

In the third expansion, I reached the *"Wisdom of the heart"*—an expanse that integrated heart with wisdom and emotion and love with knowledge, and is characterized by a sheath of glistening radiation. In this expanse, an unfamiliar urge awoke in me: to strike roots in the world and to give it my heart. In the fourth expansion, the deepening continued. I reached an *"All-embracing space."* In it, the new urge to initiate a different kind of connection with others—a genuine dialogue and a closeness free of any sense of separation—awoke even more intensely.

Eventually, in the fifth expansion, I reached the maximum I could in the present process: an expanse that, in the absence of more appropriate words, I entitled, *"The White Light."* On this plane, there was no body, no thought, and no emotion, not even love! I found myself devoid of attributes and qualities, and totally free from the world. My only wish in this expanse was to radiate the light into every space that lacked the light. Any other thing was perceived as irrelevant.

It was the most genuine self ever discovered within me, a primal and spotless self. It seemed that it existed from the beginning of time, when there was still nothing there: no body, no thoughts and no world—and yet, this was clearly a plane of great power and definitely not some sort of vacuum.

My only wish was to be, out of the knowledge that everything else simply happens of its own accord. From the plane, I looked at my personal life and saw that it could be completely harmonious, free of friction or worry, thanks to the radiation of *"The White Light"* that illuminates everything that happens. The more harmonious life is and the more background noises grow weak, the more one can unveil deeper layers and move along with new lightness. On this plane, it was clear how *"The White Light"* could illuminate everything, and thus lift any obstacle and any difficulty."

The Great Purpose of Expansion

The driving force of the expansion process—the force that propels us to perform an expansion of consciousness—is not solely the wish to be free from suffering. Actually, the longing for a release from suffering befits the earliest stages of our evolution; we might even exploit the expanded states, so as to fulfill our fantasy of escape from life. However, with the passing of time, as suffering decreases and the positive elements of our being become more and more active, we discover that there still exists a fundamental force that drives us to keep expanding.

I call this force "the urge to merge." This urge is not personal. Rather, it is the will of the great life itself as it throbs within us. It is originated from the subtle fields of the universe, and it may germinate in us, for the first time, in our mental-spiritual field, as the passion for spiritual development. My claim is that this urge is the driving force of genuine spirituality, and at the same time, it is the driving force of the tremendous evolutionary movement as we know it: the process of development for the entire universe— from the layer of physics toward the layer of chemistry, and from the layer of chemistry toward the layer of biology, and from the layer of biology to the layer of self-awareness, and from the layer of self-awareness to the subtle fields of consciousness. The cosmos itself is driven by the urge to merge, which is the persistent urge for the abolition of limitations and the increasing absorption of the partial into the greater whole; the creation of new, more complex structures, alongside the breakthrough of limitations, which aims at reaching the next step.

This is how contemporary theorist of spiritual evolution Beatrice Bruteau depicts the nature of evolution: "There is a basic urgency in life to grow, to expand, and to become new and renewed. We might even say that the very meaning of being alive is to constantly be in the process of becoming a new creation. This happens on small scales with every biological form we know, and it happens on a large scale in the universe as a whole. At least one contemporary view of the cosmos sees it as one huge, dynamic, evolving being that passes through a series of stages in which its forms and internal relations assume ever-new patterns. Some theorists of evolution point out that with each succeeding stage of development, the complexity of the patterns is increased. So evolution is the passage in time from simpler organizational forms to more complex organizational forms, carrying with it an increase of consciousness, which means a sense of unity in the organized entity. Now, this process is usually thought of as advancing by a series of small steps. But sometimes there is a Great Step. Great Steps occur when the cosmic organization goes to another level of complexity. It does this by uniting elements of the preceding level... All of evolution has progressed by a series of creative unions. More complex and more conscious beings are formed by the union of less complex and less conscious elements with one another. Subatomic particles unite to form atoms, atoms unite to form molecules, molecules unite to form cells, and cells unite to form organisms. This same pattern of creating something new, something more complex and more conscious, by the union of the less complex and less conscious recurs at each of these levels. It is because we can look back and see the pattern, see it recurring, that... we can legitimately extrapolate and project the pattern into the future, looking forward to another creative union in which *we* will be the uniting elements."

Everything is filled with a desire to spread and expand, a desire to no longer be a confined structure but to dissolve into a more complex and less limited structure. Everything aspires to move toward a more complex, conscious and intelligent level of existence. This is the force that eventually drove the human species to detach from the planetary stream and to start developing a capacity for thought and contemplation; this is the force responsible for any astounding "evolutionary leap" that has occurred in the universe, and therefore, it is the force that brought about the leap from monkey to human, and it is the one that will increasingly bring about the leap from an ordinary human consciousness to a vast and illuminated consciousness.

Whenever we feel the desire to perform an expansion, it means that the more partial and limited seeks to shatter its boundaries and assimilate into the broader and more wholesome. When we allow the desire for expansion to release any and all limits, it leads us to the complete realization of the potential of our consciousness: revelation of the five fields, settlement in them and finally, Enlightenment. The sole interest of the urge to merge, in its expression through the human consciousness, is to go beyond the limit, to always discover what lies beyond the present level of consciousness and realize, more and more, that which is more wholesome and inclusive.

Therefore, fundamentally, the expansion process of the White Light is but a way to awaken the urge itself, a way to ignite its action in man. It is a disintegration and a re-integration of each and every level, an inclusion and transcendence of and beyond any possible stage, a continuous movement for the negation of the known and an eager question that sets its gaze upon the threshold of the unknown. In this sense, the urge to merge does not only fulfill the longing, which resides in our depths, for our primordial being that knew no limitations and restrictions, but it is also the very urge of the future: it aims at the construction of a more and more complex, intelligent and aware consciousness and life; it aims at the expansion of life itself and the creation of a new future.

A great advantage of the urge to merge is also that it maintains a persistent level of positive evolutionary tension—the tension that stands between a potential and a further fulfillment. We might fail to understand the meaning of the spiritual journey and fail to think that its purpose is to lead us, eventually, to a state of the cessation of all tension and absolute tranquility, yet we should be very cautious about the possible cessation of the positive tension of life. Life has its own positive "frustration" and its own positive "ambition," which are evolutionary by their very nature and are discovered precisely as our experience of life becomes more positive and peaceful and as the urge to merge turns into the driving force of our being.

Expansion and the Future of Humanity

Whenever I pass through groups of participants in a White Light workshop while they practice the expansion process, the experience is undeniable: the large hall and the practice rooms are flooded with the powerful vibration of the subtle fields of consciousness. At such moments, I usually smile to myself contentedly since it is obvious to me not only that the lives and consciousnesses of the participants are about to change as a result of the direct contact with the fields but also that something in the planetary fabric itself and in the collective human consciousness will transform, at least to some extent, as a result of each such workshop. In the end, one may definitely assume that every breakthrough in the field of consciousness, even if it takes place on a rather small scale, makes it much more possible for everyone else to break through—for instance, by creating a new level of activity in the brain.

The somewhat disputable phenomenon referred to as the "hundredth monkey effect" may serve as an example of this. Many are acquainted with the reports of the mid-seventies about the observations of Japanese scientists in regard to the contagious emergence of behavioral patterns amongst monkeys. The claim is that during the year of 1952, the scientists had watched the activity of macaque monkeys on the Japanese island of Koshima. They had found out that a few monkeys had developed the habit of washing sweet potatoes, and gradually, this habit had adhered to the younger generation of the monkeys. Wondrously, it seemed that, from the moment the habit accumulated a kind of momentum amongst the island monkeys, it spread out to other surrounding islands and ignited a similar behavior there, too. The biochemist Rupert Sheldrake uses this case as possible supporting evidence for the existence of fields (which he himself entitles "morphogenetic fields"). Ever since, this story has turned into a popular example people use to demonstrate the ability of an idea or a state of consciousness to spread throughout the human population as soon as it gains ground within a sufficient number of people, and consequently, to turn into a natural and immediate capacity of the general consciousness.

Naturally, this well-known case is refutable, and yet, in a very interesting manner, we have observed this phenomenon being actualized in the White Light method also. At the first stages of the dissemination of the method, the process of expansion was perceived to be challenging in the eyes of many, and people had to make their way through the process with exceptional effort and concentration—to such an extent that the instructors of the method used to employ, in the first sessions, techniques for relaxation and mental flexibility, so that the student would be able to actually enter into the process of expansion in the following sessions. Strangely, today—more than five years since the process of expansion was first developed—there is hardly any person that finds it difficult to carry out the process; teenagers, the elderly, men and women, spiritual seekers and businessmen, almost everyone expands without difficulty and arrives at the mental-spiritual field. In my careful estimation, this does not stem from the confidence we have gathered over time—after all, the forms of the techniques have remained as they were at the very beginning, and the instructors simply read them out—but rather from the contagious spread of the habit of expansion in the collective fields.

The consciousness of most people has not yet developed sufficiently to reach the point in which they can consider the personal liberation process they go through within the broader context of the evolution of consciousness and the future of humanity. Hence, at this stage, the majority of the people undergoing White Light processes partake, unknowingly, in an extremely vast event: the formation of a more complex, intelligent and aware consciousness that is destined to play a crucial role in designing the future of mankind and the entire planet.

The fact that, within many, the capacity to contact the subtle fields of consciousness is developing, is, in itself, a tremendous evolutionary leap for us as the human species. For thousands of years, interaction with the subtle fields was considered the outcome of combining an enormous self-effort—many years of meditation and esoteric spiritual practice—and a divinely-originated "grace." Now, people lacking any experience in meditation and even any previous spiritual knowledge, penetrate, with extreme ease, into highly profound states of consciousness and being and, moreover, learn how to apply these states to different needs.

The emergence of the subtle fields as obvious layers of human consciousness and the discovery of their practical aspects bear highly significant implications. Among other things, we can include the ending of psychological suffering and the emergence of a post-psychological era. But above all, the activity of the fields might remold the human brain and shift it from its current level of functioning—thinking—to a new level of functioning that may be regarded as "listening" and "insight." Such a brain may turn into a gateway to creative and holistic solutions, to the end of the conflictual dynamic of the world and to the rise of unknown pathways of intelligence.

With the emergence of the subtle fields within many consciousnesses, the urge to merge might also awaken, more and more, as a central driving force in the actions of humans. The urge to merge is the future-constructing and development-encouraging element within us; it is the most profound positive force to drive man into action—the will to infinitely grow through the positive tension of life. The urge to merge propels us toward an ever-increasing expansion in all dimensions of our being and life, and through it, the excited and ecstatic consciousness can unveil and fulfill new potential for the human experience, new possibilities for transcendence beyond the limitations of our present experience of life. There is never a real limit to the extent to which our consciousness, heart, brain, thoughts and emotions can evolve and expand, and unlike the cynical worldview, on no account can one claim that everything has already happened: there is always something new to discover beyond the present border.

Yet, perhaps the most crucial change of them all, which the discovery of subtle fields holds within it, is the rising of absolute self-authority. The expansion of the self-identity along the fields evokes a sense of increasing responsibility for all that is—after all, through the expansion of the identity, we find out that the entire cosmos is concealed within the seed of our "I;" the universe lies within our consciousness and hence, there is no one but us. In this understanding that there is no power outside man, awaits not some form of megalomania, but rather full responsibility, perhaps for the first time in human history, for the shaping of our future. As soon as we abandon our dependency on external and fate-directing forces, we abandon, along with it, all hope and waiting. The direct implication is that only we can turn the world into hell - and only we can make the world a paradise.

In the subconscious of the human race, remnants of memory connections from the long periods in which the great religions molded our view of the world still survive. All great religions are founded on promise, hope and patience: whether we are waiting for the Messiah or the end of days, or trying to be "good" so as to earn a seat in the world to come or in the heavens. As a result, we still experience ourselves as victims of the vast world, wondering why there is evil in the world and if there is a God, how suffering can exist at all. Now we can awaken to the simple truth that evil and suffering are nothing but a direct outcome of a low level of consciousness, which means that evil and suffering will come to an end with a shift to a higher level of consciousness.

As our self-identity expands and becomes all-inclusive, amazing transformations take place within us until it is no longer possible to trace our formerly small and bruised personality: we awaken to an inconceivable sense of responsibility, overflowing with passion to act for the betterment of the whole and for the sake of the future. We also start recognizing ourselves as a source of grace, abundance, wisdom and love. We experience within us the arousal (out of the fourth, cosmic-soul field) of urges of creation and participation in the design of the courses of life, and we realize that, if indeed there is some God out there, His wish is exactly this—that we should become co-creating partners in the enterprise of creation and that we should, more and more, take on our shoulders the mission of consciously leading life as a whole. In religious terms, the son should become a father himself one day.

Only the development of a self-identity can allow the emergence of a new self that has nothing to do with the self which preceded it— the same old self that turned the world into such a difficult and conflicted arena. On a small scale, we get in touch with that whenever we undergo the expansion process of "White Light for Self-Identity."

In my mind, the future of humanity is wholly dependent on the development of consciousness. It is the quality of the consciousness that determines our present state, and so, it is a determining factor in what our future will look like. Without a substantial development of consciousness, man might remain entrapped in the psychological plane as we know it, and, as a result, remain conditioned to structures of thought which are circular, conflictual and, by nature, resistant to radical change. Without a substantial development of consciousness, we will never succeed in creating the wondrous heaven that we are destined to create on this earth. This is precisely the gift of transformative spirituality, which, for some strange reason, we have become accustomed to, considering it an esoteric activity for "people in search of themselves:" it endows us with the tools to move, in the fastest way possible, toward this longed-for consciousness, which has the power to bring forth a future and a humanity of a brand new order.

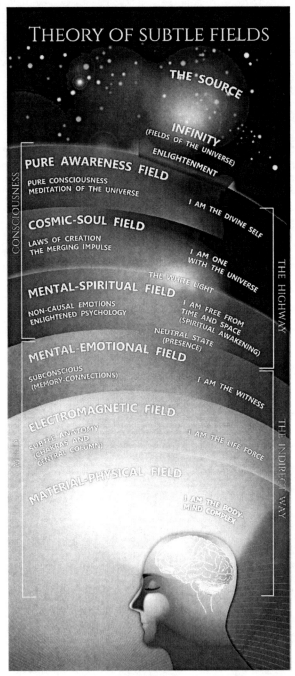

Diagram A

Diagram B

Sources

Frankl Viktor, *Man's search for meaning: an introduction to Logotherapy*, translation: Haim Isaac, Tel Aviv, Israel, Dvir, 1970.

Bruteau Beatrice, *A song that goes on singing*, WIE magazine, volume 21, 2002.

Other Books from MSI Press

365 Teacher Secrets for Parents: Fun Ways to Help Your Child Succeed in Elementary School (McKinley & Trombly)

A Believer-in-Waiting's First Encounters with God (Mahlou)

Accused! How to Help When Your Priest Is in Trouble (Jane)

Blest Atheist (Mahlou)

Creative Aging: A Baby Boomer's Guide to Successful Living (Vassiliadis & Romer)

Forget the Goal, the Journey Counts (Stites)

Joshuanism: A Path beyond Christianity (Tosto)

Lessons of Labor: One Woman's Self-Discovery through Birth and Motherhood (Julia Aziz)

Losing My Voice and Finding Another (Thompson)

Mommy Poisoned Our House Guest (S. Leaver)

Of God, Rattlesnakes, and Okra: A Preacher's Boy Tells His Growing-Up Story (Easterling)

Publishing for Smarties: How to Find a Publisher (Ham)

Syrian Folktales (M. Imady)

The Marriage Whisperer: Tips to Improve Your Relationship Overnight (Pickett)

The Rise and Fall of Muslim Civil Society (O. Imady)

The Rose and the Sword: How to Balance Your Feminine and Masculine Energies (Bach and Hucknall)

The Gospel of Damascus (O. Imady)

The Road to Damascus (E. Imady)

The Seven Wisdoms of Life: A Journey into the Chakras (Tubali)

The Widower's Guide to a New Life (Rome)

Thoughts without a Title (Henderson)

Understanding the People around You (Filatova)

When You're Shoved from the Right, Look to Your Left (O. Imady)

Widow: A Survival Guide for the First Year (Romer)

CPSIA information can be obtained
at www.ICGtesting.com
Printed in the USA
FFOW02n0903300715
15492FF